Private Gardens of SCOTLAND

Private Gardens of
SCOTLAND

JAMES TRUSCOTT
Photographs by Hugh Palmer

FOREWORD BY
PRINCESS ALICE,
DUCHESS OF GLOUCESTER

Harmony Books/New York

To Joyce

without whose encouragement
this book would have
remained just a dream

Photographer's Acknowledgements

I should like to thank all the owners for their
kind permission to have their gardens
photographed, and for the welcome I received
on so many occasions during a most
pleasurable year.
    The pictures are respectfully dedicated to
Miss Elizabeth Mallett F.R.P.S., pioneer of
early color photography and tireless
explorer of Scotland's West Coast.

H.P.

Text copyright © 1988 by James Truscott

Photographs copyright © 1988 by Hugh Palmer

Foreword copyright © 1988 by Princess Alice, Duchess of
Gloucester

Published in the United States by Harmony Books, a division
of Crown Publishers, Inc., 225 Park Avenue South, New York,
New York 10003.

Published in Great Britain by George Weidenfeld and Nicolson
Limited.
HARMONY and colophon are trademarks of Crown Publishers,
Inc.
Manufactured in Italy

Library of Congress Cataloging-in-Publication Data
Truscott, James.
Private gardens of Scotland/by James Truscott: photographs
by Hugh Palmer.
        p.   cm.
    Bibliography: p.
    Includes index.
    ISBN 0–517–56974–4: $50.00
    1. Gardens—Scotland.   2. Scotland—Description and
travel—1981–
I. Palmer, Hugh.   II. Title.
SB466.G75S3574   1988
712′.6′09411—dcig   88–10997 CIP
10 9 8 7 6 5 4 3 2 1
First Edition

Acknowledgements

A number of the chapters in this book are updated versions of a series of articles which first appeared under the title 'In a Garden' in the *Scottish Field* magazine between July 1985 and March 1986, and the author would like to thank the publishers, Holmes McDougall, and the editors, especially Roddy Martine, for their kind permission to reproduce them here. He would also like to thank *Scottish Ambassador* and *Country Living* magazines for their permission to reproduce updated versions of articles on Balmoral and Geilston respectively, and the staff of *Country Life* magazine for their co-operation during the writing of the manuscript.

This book could not have been published without the assistance of all the owners of the private gardens who gave permission for their privacy to be invaded, both by the author and by Hugh Palmer, the photographer. For their kind hospitality on these occasions, and for checking over the draft text on their properties, the author extends his sincere thanks, as he does to the owners of the many gardens that were visited and eventually omitted from the book owing simply to restrictions on the number of properties it was possible to include. Lack of space also prevents the individual mention here of all the owners involved, but special thanks are due to the MacMillan family, Lady Ancram and Lady Edmonstone for their enthusiastic assistance and advice, to the committee of Scotland's Gardens Scheme for their co-operation, and of course, to S.G.S.'s President, H.R.H. Princess Alice, Duchess of Gloucester, who graciously consented to write the foreword.

The author would also like to extend his thanks to the staff at Weidenfeld and Nicolson, notably Michael Dover and Wendy Dallas, for their greatly appreciated assistance in the preparation of the text, especially in the latter stages, to Hugh Palmer whose photographs contribute so much to the book, to Jim Tomlinson for his advice, and to Ruth Mackenzie for efficiently typing out the drafts.

Last, but by no means least, I would like to thank my wife, Joyce, not only for her considerable editorial skills and many helpful suggestions during the writing of this book but also for her patience, fortitude and encouragement.

J.S.T., October 1987

Contents

Foreword

There are few places in the world that boast such a variety of glorious gardens and garden settings as Scotland. The gardens so well chosen by the author and skilfully photographed, generously reflect geographic and climatic diversities: the well established and the newly formed, the formal and informal. A romantic and often stormy history, combined with the altitude of the countryside, instills in Scottish gardens a very special and unique quality, which Mr Truscott's book sets out and succeeds in capturing.

The all absorbing world of gardening is as vital now as it ever was in the pre-war days of the Grand Garden. How fortunate that most of those private gardens share their pleasures and their secrets with so many appreciative visitors under the auspices of Scotland's Gardens Scheme, of which I am proud to have been President since 1937.

To those who know little of Scotland or her gardens, this book will prove a delight and a revelation; to those as yet uninformed with this aspect of Scottish heritage, an insight, and to the gardeners of Scotland an inspiration. It is their knowledge and enthusiasm which they bring to so many visitors that makes the writing of this foreword a special pleasure for me.

Alice

HRH PRINCESS ALICE,
DUCHESS OF GLOUCESTER

Preface

Statues by the Italian sculptor Antonio Bonazza on a Hebridean Island; a Chilean flamebush by a water garden designed by Japanese gardeners and overlooked by a ruined castle in Aberdeenshire; the grounds of a fairytale castle in a secluded valley at the foot of the Campsie Fells, only fifteen miles from Glasgow city centre; tender plants growing in a formal garden inspired by Versailles, on a latitude similar to Greenland; Himalayan rhododendrons in a highland glen: these and many other surprises and delights await the perceptive visitor to Scotland who cares to spend some time exploring the glories of her private gardens.

This book is not, however, intended to be a gazetteer, or a definitive or scholarly work on Scottish gardens. Neither does it attempt to present a highly specialized horticultural or botanical view of the subject, nor indeed a description of the 'Top Twenty' properties in the Scots gardening league. The appreciation of gardens should, after all, not be an academic exercise but a feast for the senses, a temporary withdrawal from humdrum everyday life into a cloistered world of scents and colours, where half-forgotten feelings of wonderment and awe can be rediscovered. This book is an attempt to transport the reader to this magical world and, by means of pictures and words, to conjure up the delights of these private Scottish gardens.

Of the twenty-three properties represented here, the majority are open for at least one day

Above: An espalier apple tree in the walled garden at Tyinghame House.

a year under Scotland's Gardens Scheme, to which more than two hundred and fifty gardens belong. There are of course innumerable others which do not subscribe to this scheme, and choosing examples to reflect the spectrum of Scottish gardens was not an easy task. The final choice was based upon three criteria. Firstly, geographical diversity. The gardens included range from Arbigland, on the Solway Firth in the south, to Dunrobin Castle on the Moray Firth, not far from John O'Groats, and from Torosay Castle on the Hebridean island of Mull to Tyninghame in the east. The book has, furthermore, been divided into three broad geographical areas representing in general terms areas with similar types of topography and climate and correspondingly similar peak times for viewing. There are, of course, exceptions to the rule, but these divisions do provide an overall guide to the sort of gardens that can be found in a particular area, and the periods when visitors are most likely to see them at their best. The second criterion was garden type. Although the geographical and topographical situation of a garden can restrict the range of plant species which can be grown there, design and layout are as infinitely varied as the landscape of Scotland itself. Garden types can, nevertheless, be very roughly grouped together, and this book describes as many different examples of particular types as possible, as well as some which completely defy categorization. Finally, size was an important factor; the gardens chosen range from one acre to a hundred and fifty acres, representing a complete cross-section from the intimate to the grandiose.

The civic boundaries in Scotland have been changed in recent years and now comprise large regions subdivided into districts, which have replaced the old counties. The current official regional names have been used in the contents list and chapter headings, but the old county names have been used in the text as the history of many of these properties is inextricably linked with them. In some cases as many as six old counties have been absorbed into one new region, and use of the old name denotes variations in topography, climate, soil and other features that are characteristic of individual counties but not common to the entire region.

Each garden has been shaped by its owners and, in some cases, by generations of owners, and their resolve to preserve their creation for future generations has led to an increasing number of owners forming private trusts, by which they hope to ensure the garden's survival in the face of spiralling maintenance costs. Four such gardens are presented here. They have all remained private in character, and in every case the former owners, who cared for them for so long, are still an important guiding force, usually acting as trustees or directors. Thus, although their ownership may have changed, these gardens have retained much of their original appearance.

Exploring a garden is a very personal experience, and this is a personal journey through just some of the splendours and surprises which await the fortunate visitor to Scotland's private gardens.

Further details of opening dates and times of many of the gardens featured in this book can be obtained from: Scotland's Gardens Scheme, 31 Castle Terrace, Edinburgh EH1 2EL

Left: Huge yew archways on either side of the series of grass terraces leading to the water garden at Rossie Priory.

Introduction

Scotland: A brief resumé of its geography, topography and climate

To Scottish readers it may seem unnecessary to reiterate that in scenic, historical and cultural terms Scotland is still a country apart from England and that it has developed along widely divergent lines. Scotland's gardens too have developed a uniquely Scottish identity. There are similarities and parallels with gardens elsewhere in the British Isles and Europe, of course, but even foreign influences are given a Scottish twist when set against the history and rugged terrain that makes up this most northerly and arguably most beautiful region of Great Britain.

Scotland is a more extensive country than is commonly realized: it is as far from Gretna Green to John O'Groats as it is from Gretna Green to London; and from the Kyle of Lochalsh on the west coast to Peterhead on the east is about the same distance as from London to Sheffield. It is a country of great contrasts in scenery too. Everyone is prepared for the mountainous highland scenery of the west coast and the Cairngorms in the north-east, but not always for the rich, rolling agricultural lands of Ayrshire, Aberdeen and Angus, the mellow, wooded valleys of the Borders, the open splendour of the Firths of Solway, Clyde and Forth, and the Hebridean islands with their white beaches, looking on a sunny day more like South Sea islands than Scottish ones.

Moreover Scotland extends further north than is generally appreciated, its most northerly reaches lying only a couple of degrees south of Leningrad, Greenland and Alaska. The fact that gardens can flourish here at all is due largely to the proximity of the sea, whose benign influence is felt particularly on the west coast, where the North Atlantic drift, the northern arm of the Gulf Stream, has an ameliorating effect. Inland, however, it is a different story: away from the sea, winter temperatures can plummet to minus 25°C, and snow is a common occurrence. The summer too is noticeably shorter than in the south of England; frosts can occur until early June and start again in late August, and spring can be a very fleeting season.

There is also a sharp dichotomy in climate between west and east. The west, generally milder and wetter, is prone to assault from the prevailing south-westerlies. The east is significantly drier but still suffers from the cold eastern winds blowing off the Continental land mass. In spring and early summer these icy blasts can often wither buds and newly opened leaves alike.

From this it sounds as though gardening in Scotland is an uphill struggle fought by relatively few, but this is clearly not the case, as will be amply demonstrated by the gardens illustrated here. Not only has the challenge been taken up by thousands of Scottish gardeners over the past few centuries but conditions of climate and topography have been used to advantage in creating some of the most unusual, spectacular and varied gardens to be found anywhere in the world.

The formal gardens of Scotland and their use of surrounding features

If there is a recognizable school of gardening that is uniquely Scottish, it could perhaps be defined as working *with* nature rather than against her. Even in early times, when formality in garden layout was pre-eminent and symmetry was considered the key to good design, features in the surrounding landscape were used as distant eye-catchers, their wildness and asymmetry serving as a foil to the formality of the foreground, almost as if they were part of the garden. Sir William Bruce of Kinross, in the mid-seventeenth century, used the distant Bass Rock, a rocky protrusion off the east Lothian coast, as the focal point of the main axis of Balcaskie House in Fife. Similarly, the ruin of Leven Castle, on an island in the middle of Loch Leven, was used to terminate the view along the main walk at Kinross House. At Arbigland, near Dumfries, the distant hills of the Lake District across the Solway Firth are framed by the south-facing gateway of the walled garden, which dates from the eighteenth century.

Sometimes, if there were no natural features to focus on, an eye-catcher would be created, such as at Drummond in Perthshire, although even here, in one of Scotland's most formal gardens, the topography itself has been exploited to give the visitor an aerial view of the garden from the top of the steep slope on which the castle stands, a device used to similar advantage at Dunrobin Castle in Sutherland. At Castle Kennedy near Stranraer, the ruins of the old castle were used as a focal point and eye-catcher from the entrance to the gardens and from various other points, so that they form a central axis. This practice was sometimes used in reverse, especially in the seventeenth century, and was known by the French term *patte d'oie*: each vista, walk or alley radiated from a central point and terminated in some feature of interest – a hill, a castle or an artificial eye-catcher.

The technique of incorporating views of the surrounding landscape into the design of the garden is not unique to the seventeenth and eighteenth centuries, however. At Monteviot, in the Borders, the River Teviot and the fields beyond are the focal point of the main axis of the formal river garden, laid out in the 1960s by Percy Cane. At Greywalls in East Lothian, the distant Lammermuir Hills are framed in an opening in the wall that terminates the main axis of the garden, which was designed by the famous Edwardian partnership of Sir Edwin Lutyens and Gertrude Jekyll.

The landscape movement in Scotland

Clearly then, the formal and the informal are by no means mutually exclusive in Scotland, and indeed in many cases the juxtaposition of one with the other strengthens both. But what of the landscape movement, which had such far-reaching effects on gardens in England and elsewhere? The truth is that with a few exceptions, such as Manderston and Mellerstain in the rolling hillsides of the Borders, the concept of the landscape garden as practised in England by Capability Brown and William Kent – that of undulating hillsides, semi-natural tree clumps and serpentine lakes – never transferred very successfully to Scotland. What did develop, however, was a very Scottish form of landscape gardening which took its inspiration from the existing surroundings, adapting the concept in a wholly individual way to Scottish topography and conditions. This form of landscape gardening was first advocated by Lord Kames, a contemporary of Brown, in the mid-eighteenth century, and has survived to this day.

Woodland gardens, wild gardens and glen gardens

The trend towards wild and woodland gardens during the latter half of the last century was greatly encouraged by the arrival of new and exotic plants from abroad, brought back

Right: Both the landscape
and the climate at
Arduaine are somewhat
Himalayan in character.

ner John Loudon, is magnificently illustrated by the gardens of Kildrummy Castle, Crarae Glen and Arduaine.

Plant collections

Another feature of middle to late nineteenth-century gardening was plant collections. It became fashionable to collect exotic plants from abroad, and there was considerable friendly rivalry among plantsmen to grow the latest and most unusual plants from seed, and to hybridize them. Most large gardens had their own arboretum or pinetum, probably the best example in Scotland being the famous pinetum at Scone Palace in Perthshire. Many of its conifers, planted over a hundred years ago, are now enormous: one of the Sitka spruces is about 160 feet high. A more recent plant collection is that at Achamore House, on the Isle of Gigha, where earlier this century Sir James Horlick amassed an unrivalled collection of large-leaved rhododendrons, camellias and pieris species and hybrids. Many garden owners on the west coast exchanged new varieties and in the process helped to build up one another's collections.

Revival of the formal garden

Alongside the woodland gardens and semi-wild landscape gardens, there was also a growing movement towards a revival of the formal garden, notably in the latter half of the last century and the early part of this century. Torosay, Finlaystone and Carnell to the west, and Manderston, the re-designed Drummond gardens, Rossie Priory, Tyninghame, Dunrobin and Balmoral to the east and north, all have formal gardens which date from this intensely active period of garden building. Even though many of them were influenced by French and Italian ideas, their relationship with the surrounding landscape – as the gardens of the seventeenth century had been – is peculiarly Scottish, even if only in terms of the contrast between the formality of their design and the informality of the scenery. The

by Scottish plant collectors – Francis Masson from Aberdeen, Thomas Drummond from Forfar, George Forrest from Falkirk and Robert Fortune from Edinburgh. Their names will be recognized by many readers as so many garden plants have been named after them, such as *Pieris formosa forrestii*, *Acer platanoides* 'Drummondii' and *Rhododendron fortunei*. Before their arrival the choice of plants was limited to native species, and in landscape gardens plants were used more to enclose an area or to create mass rather than for their individual interest.

With the introduction of rhododendrons and azaleas and their hybrids, the Scottish gardener, especially on the west coast, had the perfect plants for semi-naturalized woodland, and from this impetus sprang the woodland and glen gardens which are such a marvellous and characteristic feature of the Scottish west coast today. Such plants seem almost to belong in a Caledonian setting and, indeed, Scotland's climate and topography are not at all dissimilar to those of their native homelands. Not only their vivid colours but also their sculptural leaves and bark seem to complement the dramatic surroundings. This use of exotic plants in a romantic, semi-wild setting, first pioneered by Lord Kames and developed by the early nineteenth-century landscape garde-

Left: The formal southern section of the garden contrasts with the beach and the blue Dornoch Firth beyond.

gardens at Torosay Castle, on the Isle of Mull, were designed by Sir Robert Lorimer at the turn of the century, and took the form of a series of descending Italianate terraces, the main walk being flanked by Italian statues. It is the stark contrast between this imposed formality and the wild rugged mountain landscape of Argyll behind which is one of the most exhilarating features of the garden. Other Scottish gardens have managed to combine both formal and informal schemes: at Duntreath Castle in Stirlingshire, for example, the gardens immediately around the castle are formal but informality takes over in the outer reaches of the garden so that the castle seems to belong in its picturesque valley setting, an example of the almost intuitive sensitivity to the spirit of the place that Scots gardeners have demonstrated over the years.

Herbaceous and walled gardens

The informal cottage-style garden advocated by William Robinson and Gertrude Jekyll earlier this century can be seen in herbaceous gardens throughout Scotland, and especially at Greywalls (Miss Jekyll's only Scottish garden), at Carnell and, to a greater or lesser extent, in many traditional Scottish walled gardens. The importance of shelter has always been recognized as vital to the survival of gardens north of the border and, since about the sixteenth century, protection has been provided either by walls, hedging or woodland planting, or quite often by a combination of all three. Originally walled gardens, nearly always situated some distance from the house, were used purely for growing fresh fruit, vegetables and herbs for the 'big house', a function which the majority of them still perform to this day, though to a much lesser extent. But the decorative properties of herbs, espalier apples and other fruit trees have always been appreciated by gardeners and used to good effect. Flowers first made an appearance in the walled garden in the seventeenth century, or perhaps even earlier, initially to provide cut flowers for the house but later to add colour and interest to the walled garden itself. By the eighteenth and nineteenth centuries brick was beginning to be used for walling, although quite often as a skin on the inside of a more traditional masonry wall, as some gardeners considered brick's property of heat retention to be beneficial to espalier fruits. Some walled gardens, such as at Tyninghame, even had internal heating systems. Tyninghame is also a good example of the increasingly decorative function that such gardens performed towards the end of the nineteenth century. At Brechin, curved walls, gravel walks, a garden temple and a pond have been developed over the last century and a half to produce one of the most delightful walled gardens in Scotland.

The glasshouse was also an important feature of the Victorian walled garden, once again gardeners vying with each other to grow exotic fruits and decorative plants brought back by plant collectors from all over the globe. Grapes were a favourite fruit at this time, and some, like the Tyninghame muscat grape, became locally renowned.

Current problems and future possibilities

This century has unfortunately witnessed the decline and, in some cases, the demise of many walled gardens, as the expense of upkeep has combined with a drop in the size of households and consequently in the domestic demand for fresh fruit and vegetables. The cost of maintenance and staffing has also had wider implications for the Scottish garden. The number of gardeners employed has dropped dramatically, and despite the increased use of machinery and chemicals, it has often been difficult for owners even to maintain the *status quo*. Inevitably savings have had to be made. Some changes, such as the widespread substitution of roses for Victorian bedding plants in box parterres, may be for the better. Others, such as the wholesale removal of plants and their substitution by wide expanses of grass can sometimes, though not always, detract from the overall design. A number of owners have confronted this worrying prospect of contraction and decline by opening their gardens to the public, which some may argue will destroy the very atmosphere of seclusion which makes them so attractive. Many gardens, however, especially those divided into compartments, can absorb fairly large numbers of people without losing their charm, and if it is a clear choice between this option and extinction, opening the gates to the public is certainly the lesser of two evils.

We must always remember that the art of gardening is, by its very nature, one of constant change and development, and this need not necessarily be a downward spiral. The needs and desires of each new owner are different from those of the last, and the gardens of Scotland have witnessed many changes over the past four centuries. Despite, or rather because of this, we still have an outstanding number to enjoy. Many of these gardens, as can be seen there, are actively developing and in some cases expanding, while others are content to conserve what they have with only minor changes. Every garden is, after all, a very individual creation, only kept alive by the dedication and vision of the owners and a dwindling army of gardeners; but that, after all, is what private gardening today is all about.

In the garden something of the golden age still lingers; in the warm alleys where the bees hum above the lilies and stocks, in the blue shadows where the azure butterflies look dark in the amber haze, where the lime leaves and the acacia flowers wave joyously as the West wind passes.

SIR ROBERT LORIMER
ON SCOTTISH GARDENS

The West Coast,
West Highlands & Islands

Peak periods: May to early June; middle to late October for autumn colour.

As the snow melts from the mountains and hills of west Scotland and snowdrops give way to drifts of daffodils, her gardens awake from their winter sleep to smother the crags and glens with an unrivalled display of colour.

Warmed by the Gulf Stream and the mild, wet westerlies which roll in across the Hebrides, islands and promontories such as Gigha and Arduaine come alive first, often several weeks ahead of gardens inland. In the peaty, acidic soil and sheltering woodland, large-leaved rhododendrons and their hybrids burst into cascades of bright flowers alongside pink splashes of camellia, usually more at home in the south of England. The high humidity encourages some plants to grow to enormous size, and nurtures others normally considered too tender to flourish so far north – embothrium, enkianthus, olearias, *Metrosideros lucida*, *Desfontainea spinosa*, crinodendron and several unusual species of pieris. Eucalyptus, cabbage palms, New Zealand warata trees and New Zealand flax lend an exotic air to this Scottish coastal scenery. The grand scale of the Castle Kennedy gardens, near Stranraer, cannot dwarf the magnificent tree rhododendrons, which grow here to a gigantic size, or the impressive monkey puzzle avenue, one of the finest in the country, which was laid out in the early eighteenth century.

Other surprises include one of the most significant collections of Italian garden statuary to be found outside Italy – on the terraces of Torosay Castle.

Many of the gardens are examples of an art at which the Scots excel, capitalizing on the existence of a wild and romantic setting by judiciously planting unusual and colourful specimens to create a garden which looks and feels at once natural and exotic. Crarae Glen is particularly impressive, with hybrid rhododendrons, candelabra primulas and blue Himalayan poppies lining the banks of a craggy highland glen which echoes with the crashing of waterfalls. Although rhododendrons and azaleas are an important element of the spring gardens of the west coast, some places make their impact in other ways: Geilston, overlooking the Clyde estuary, does have an attractive little glen garden full of rhododendrons, but is also notable for its beautiful rock garden studded with all kinds of dwarf conifers, ericas and callunas. Carnell, in the heart of Burns country, reaches its peak at the end of July, when the herbaceous border in the sunken garden is a stunning kaleidoscope of colour; here the formal is cleverly combined with the informal around a linear pool backed by another fascinating rock garden and many specimens of giant lily.

From Arbigland on the Solway Firth to Finlaystone on the Clyde estuary, and northwards to Torosay on Mull, the gardens along the spectacular western coast are an infinite source of surprise and delight.

Above: A typically naturalistic clearing planted with exotic specimens at Crarae.

Previous page: A border at Arduaine in Strathclyde.

Left: A statuesque group
of *Gunnera manicata* at
Arduaine.

Torosay Castle

ISLE OF MULL, STRATHCLYDE

Owner: Mr Christopher James

Above: A decorative stone staircase runs down the wall supporting the upper terrace. Below lies a bed of variegated hostas edged in box.

Opposite: A view from the rock garden – restored since 1979 – towards one of the gazebos on the upper, or fountain terrace.

It is often said that a garden and a house are the sum total of the people who live in it, and the magnificent garden at Torosay is a tribute not only to its recent owners but also to their forebears. Since 1972, when Torosay Castle was first opened to the public by the Hon. Mrs Jaquetta James and her husband, David Guthrie-James, an ever-increasing number of 'guests' (up to thirty thousand a year) have been welcomed to the garden, many of whom appreciate the hospitality and friendly atmosphere so much that they regularly return.

Torosay's Gaelic name, Torr Rasach, means 'hill covered with shrubs' and is still apt today. In the 1820s the land was owned by the Duke of Argyll who sold it to the Macquaries of Ulva, and they in turn to a Colonel Campbell of Possil. A small Georgian house stood here then, and the walled garden dates from this period. In the 1850s this building was demolished, and the Edinburgh architect David Bryce designed the present house, completed in 1858. It came into the Guthrie family in 1865, and by legacy into the hands of the late David Guthrie-James's grandfather, Walter Murray Guthrie, in 1897. A rough grassy slope with a few monkey puzzle trees then separated the house from the walled garden, beyond which was a woodland walk. At the turn of the century Murray Guthrie engaged the Edwardian landscape architect Sir Robert Lorimer to design and lay out a series of descending Italianate terraces to link the house with the walled garden, and at the same time the statue

walk was created, forming the major axis of the garden. This runs from the south side of the castle, down the steps of the lion terrace and through the centre of the walled garden to Duart Bay. The nineteen statues are by Antonio Bonazza (1698–1765), an Italian sculptor well known for his religious statuary, and they now constitute the most important collection of eighteenth-century sculpture outside Italy. The statues, which have recently been cleaned and restored, represent artisan figures – gardeners, gamekeepers and vendors – and also some female figures such as a lady with her dog and a rather mysterious woman in a cloak. They were brought from the garden of a derelict villa near Padua and, weighing three-quarters of a ton each, were shipped as ballast in a tramp steamer from Genoa to Glasgow, and thence by puffer (a local steam cargo ship) from Glasgow to Mull. They now contribute greatly to the formal enchantment of the terraced gardens, which are such a contrast to the wild informal landscape of Mull, Morvern and the mountains of the west that form their backdrop. The statues are set among magnificent rhododendrons and azaleas, fuchsias, *Acer palmatum* 'Dissectum Atropurpureum', deutzia, and fine specimens of *Cornus capitata* and embothrium, the Chilean flame bush. The latter was accidentally shot in lieu of a rabbit in 1964, but this 'pruning' must have been beneficial to the plant as it has prospered greatly ever since. On the three top terraces, the castle terrace, the fountain terrace and the lion terrace, are finely stocked herbaceous borders which are a riot of colour from spring until autumn. The distinctive balustraded fountain terrace has robust stone gazebos at each corner, which dominate the lion terrace below and open onto the stone staircases which lead down to it. One gazebo houses an excellent exhibition on the geology of Mull.

But there is another side to Torosay Castle gardens: like a series of satellites, the water garden, eucalyptus walk, rock garden and Japanese garden ring the main formal garden. They are hidden from it for the most part by a shield of mainly deciduous trees, and the

visitor at once realizes what sets this garden apart from many others in equally exposed locations. The usual rhododendrons and azaleas are here, with their welcome splashes of colour in early summer, though they do not dominate the garden, and there are the typically Victorian *Thuja plicata*, *Abies grandis* and *Pinus sylvestris*. But the great surprise, as one strolls towards the water garden, is the preponderance of elms, beeches, limes, oaks, horse chestnuts and many other deciduous trees more usually associated with the wooded glades of parts of lowland Scotland and England than an exposed Hebridean island.

A water garden laid out by Murray Guthrie was reinstated by his son-in-law, the late Colonel Miller, in the 1960s. The still pool, reflecting the deciduous trees which overhang it, is populated by some rather demanding ducks which sometimes wander as far as the car park in search of food. Apart from various species of iris, hosta and candelabra primula, the water garden is bordered by philadelphus, desfontania, enkianthus, pieris, euphorbia and a large clump of bamboo, all encouraged by the warmth of the Gulf Stream. Beyond is a grove of eucalyptus and leptospermum planted by Colonel Miller, which have also benefitted from the local climate judging by their size and health; they form a striking and unusual frame to the wild mountainous country behind.

Another of Colonel Miller's inspirations was the Japanese garden. This welcome addition to Torosay uses the Japanese principle of 'borrowed landscape', its simple arrangement of gravel, rocks and water acting as a perfect foil to the view of Duart Bay, Duart Castle, Ben Nevis and the other mountains beyond. The central feature of the garden itself is the red-painted Japanese bridge and the beautiful lily pond which, by reflecting its surroundings and the sky above, seems to create a feeling of unity and harmony. Small *Acer palmatum*, *Acer palmatum* 'Dissectum' and various dwarf pines accord with the garden's simplicity and restraint in being used sparingly and positioned with care.

Nearby is the rock garden, the only part of the garden kept going through the war by Mr Guthrie-James's grandmother, although it became overgrown after her death in 1945. Since 1979, it has been lovingly restored to its former glory by Jaquetta James, complete with a central pool and little paths which wind in and out among the rock plants. The most spectacular feature of this side of the garden, however, is a magnificent *Phormium tenax* which adds a strikingly exotic flourish. The lion terrace, so called because of the two

Below: The Japanese Garden uses the principle of 'borrowed landscape' to incorporate the view of Duart Castle and the mountains beyond into its overall design.

Right: Nineteen stone statues by Antonio Bonazza constitute the most important collection of eighteenth-century Italian sculpture outside Italy.

Opposite: This mysterious cloaked figure is just one of a number of statues of artisans – a notable feature of the garden.

engaging marble lions, Smiler and Growler, which crouch at either end of it, is supported by a huge stone retaining wall which collapsed in the 1950s but was rebuilt over the twenty years that followed.

The garden now extends to about eleven acres, and whereas in the 1930s a total of six gardeners were employed to look after it, Alex MacFadyen is now the only full-time gardener – not including Jaquetta James herself; another gardener works here in the summer months only, when the workload is heaviest, and two local people help on a part-time basis. Because of the closely-spaced herbaceous planting in the terrace gardens, hand weeding is necessary, although chemicals are used on the paths and walks.

It was the construction of the pier at nearby Craignure in 1964 which opened up the possibility of subsidizing the upkeep of the gardens by the admission of visitors, and Torosay now makes a popular day's excursion from Oban and even Glasgow. The new road, although single track, replaces one with grass in the middle, and links have been further improved by the construction of a narrow-gauge railway to the castle from Craignure. Twice a day, when a boat, train and busload arrive simultaneously, as many as a hundred and fifty people pass through the gate in half an hour.

The Churchills, relatives of the Guthrie-James family, have been frequent visitors to the castle; indeed it was here that Sir Winston Churchill killed his first stag. Vice Admiral Prince Louis of Battenburg, father of Earl Mountbatten, stayed here in 1909, and King George of Greece was a regular visitor.

Torosay Castle is still very much a family home, and the family tradition is maintained by Jaquetta James's son, Christopher, who now – after the death of his father – oversees the running of the estate. Its informal atmosphere, combined with the splendour of the Italianate terraced gardens and stately statue-lined walkways, leaves a vivid and lasting impression. The first banks of snowdrops, the rich colours of the rhododendrons in May and June, the midsummer shrubs and herbaceous borders, and the autumn colours reflected in clear pools surrounded by water-loving plants, make this truly a garden for all seasons, and the warmth of Torosay's welcome encourages one to feel very much a guest rather than a visitor.

TOROSAY CASTLE GARDENS are open all year round, sunrise to sunset.

Location: Craignure, Isle of Mull, $1\frac{1}{2}$ miles. Steam railway from Craignure. Steamers daily from Oban, or Lochaline–Fishnish ferry, then 7 miles south on A849.

Opposite: Looking up towards the castle from the middle terrace the magnificent display of rhododendrons and azaleas is breathtaking.

Below: Red candelabra primulas and variegated manna grass thrive on the edge of the water garden.

Arduaine

OBAN, STRATHCLYDE

Owners: Mr H. C. and Mr E. A. T. Wright

Above: Candelabra primulas grow in profusion beside the paths in the lower parts of the garden.

Opposite: A charming water garden has been constructed where the springs emerge – a series of interconnecting pools bordered by all manner of water-loving plants.

Although renowned throughout Scotland and indeed the world for its rhododendron collection, Arduaine, (pronounced Are-dew-en-ie) offers the discerning visitor an experience unique to this rocky peninsula on the Argyll coast.

The land was purchased by James Arthur Campbell, a tea planter, in 1898. It overlooks the glorious sweep of Asknish Bay, with the Inner Hebrides as a backdrop and the garden enjoys a mild microclimate. The North Atlantic drift, extremely high rainfall, and the shelter afforded by a rocky crag, which offers sufficient protection to make a garden but not enough to form a frost hollow, are very local conditions (even a few miles inland snow and frost are much more common) but they are almost identical to those found in the Himalayan foothills, the native habitat of many rhododendrons. All there was here in the 1890s were four oak trees and extensive bogland, but once a shelterbelt of larch had been planted it became an ideal spot to grow the rare and tender rhododendrons and other plants for which Arduaine has since become famous. It would be wrong, however, to think of it simply as a woodland garden; in fact, the woodland was not developed until the 1920s. The origins of the garden lie in the lower area of ground, towards what used to be Arduaine House. Now the Loch Melfort Hotel, this fine house, built by James Campbell at the turn of the century, has been purposely left unobstructed by any planting so as to take full advantage of the breathtaking views across the bay.

Next to the hotel, a grassy path, its informality and openness a dramatic contrast to the more enclosed, domestic character of the garden, leads under the overhanging boughs of some venerable *Prunus* 'Kanzan' trees to a small iron gate where the evergreen *Griselinia littoralis*, normally a medium-sized shrub, has grown to a considerable size.

Arduaine was originally laid out as a semi-formal garden, with shrub borders, a pond, a greenhouse and a vegetable garden. In the 1920s, before James Campbell's death, the woodland garden came into being, many of the rhododendrons being grown from seed (*R. zeylanicum* seed arrived from Ceylon in a chest of tea). In its heyday six gardeners and numerous other estate workers were employed here, but under Sir Bruce Campbell and his son, Major Ian Campbell, as on many estates the cost of keeping gardeners became prohibitive, and the woodland area, encouraged by the mild wet climate, grew too dense, choking out the plants beneath. It eventually became unmanageable, and in 1971 the estate was split up. Fortunately for the garden, and indeed for subsequent visitors, ownership passed to two brothers, Edmund and Harry Wright. Although they still own a nursery in Essex, Scotland has long been their adopted homeland. Their decision to move to Arduaine was clinched when they discovered that the garden had two springs of clear water – far superior to peaty highland water for making a good pot of tea!

The rescue of the garden then began in earnest, starting with the lower part, nearest to the entrance. On the left, *Olearia macrodonta major* from New Zealand, with unusual serrated leaves, blends with less unusual but nonetheless colourful shrubs such as *Cotoneaster horizontalis*, blue and pink hydrangeas, *Berberis darwinii* and numerous dwarf rhododendrons. Off the main gravel path to the left, the Wright brothers have used trees planted by earlier owners as the basic structure for a most attractive semi-formal

garden. A pool at its centre is overhung by the gnarled branches of some extremely old *Cupressus macrocarpa* and *Cedrus atlantica*, and bordered by clumps of hosta, the giant sculptural leaves of *Gunnera manicata* and *Bergenia cordifolia*; the aptly named elephant's ears and the American skunk cabbage lend an exotic air to this part of the garden, enhanced by the spiky leaves of *Phormium tenax*, the peeling bark of eucalyptus trees and the white plumes of pampas grass. The mature atlantic cedars, Scots pine and American oaks planted by the original members of the Campbell family add considerable depth and character to this area, which seems to have more in common with some exotic island than a peninsula on the west coast of Scotland. This feeling of being in an idyllic island setting is underlined by frequent glimpses of the sea through gaps in the trees, the constant cry of gulls and the salty tang of the sea breeze.

Where the springs emerge the Wrights have made a charming water garden in which a gently trickling stream falls into a descending series of pools bordered by beds of moisture-loving plants – ferns, hostas and candelabra primulas – with groups of dwarf rhododendrons, azaleas and unusual shrubs such as *Olearia insignis*, a white-flowering evergreen from New Zealand, on higher ground above. They have recently opened up a view down the length of the ponds by removing some large overhanging rhododendrons and other shrubs that were past their prime. Paths have been altered and new beds created, planted with more hostas, lilies, primulas and astilbes, whose plumes catch the sunlight, and earlier in the year the large clear blue flowers of the Himalayan poppy, *Meconopsis betonicifolia*, make a spectacular display. The magnificent cedar of Lebanon has been cleared of surrounding escallonias and other shrubs which masked its outline, and beneath it a new bed has been planted with low-growing plants.

Buzzards soar in the sky above the craggy rockface which protects the garden, and below are the smooth green lawns that once supported the vegetable garden, surrounded

Left: The lower part of the garden was laid out in the early part of this century: the borders of the main path now contain many interesting specimens – olearias and dwarf rhododendrons, for example.

Left: A damp corner of the water garden with ferns and sphagnum moss.

by the colours and textures of herbaceous plants and shrubs which climb up the crevices of the rocks. Since the erection of a rabbit fence the herbaceous borders are blooming better than ever.

James Arthur Campbell introduced many of the more unusual plants that grow so well here today, such as the massive *Rhododendron auriculatum*, whose white flowers scent the woodland in August, and the twenty-five-foot *R. giganteum*, its vast leaves carried on heavy branches. It first produced its magnificent purple flowers here in 1936, the first such plant to do so in the western hemisphere. The

Opposite: The grandeur of the garden and its coastal setting can be fully appreciated from this fenced ledge beneath the overhanging cliff.

woodland, the more sheltered part of the garden, has some of the most tender, rare and unusual rhododendrons to be found in the United Kingdom. Here, the convoluted form of *R. sinogrande* reaches about thirty feet, and the normally tender *R. griffithianum* seems to flourish under the sheltering boughs of larch, sycamore, beech and cryptomeria. Close to these large-leaved specimens, the unusual *R. oulotrichum*, with small leaves and slender branches, forms an elegant contrast. And not only do rhododendrons thrive here: bamboo,

hydrangea, magnolia and griselinia, holly and pieris all vie for space and light. In a central clearing edged by eucalyptus trees a hundred feet tall clumps of gunnera grow, with hosta groups in the wetter spots. Clearing the denser parts of the wood, creating new glades, planting and transplanting is a continuing process in the development of the garden.

Past the Wrights' cottage, which is set in a picturesque clearing, one emerges from the dense woodland to a sudden and breathtaking view spreading below. From a fenced ledge beneath the overhanging cliff, the grandeur of the garden and its coastal setting can be absorbed at leisure, and even the profusion of ericacae, berberis and cotoneaster take second place. The eastern end of the cliff, cleared of the spindly and unimportant trees and shrubs that were growing there, has been completely replanted with more interesting specimens, and the recent upgrading of paths and handrails has made this worthwhile climb less daunting to the unsteady. From this 'gallery' a winding stairway takes the intrepid visitor back to terra firma and the old vegetable garden, where the tour began.

Edmund Wright, when he has time to take a break from the manual upkeep of the garden, is Secretary and Treasurer of the Scottish Rhododendron Society. He is keen to point out that Arduaine is very much a plantsman's garden, and although the three thousand or more annual visitors, most of them parties of horticulturists from all over the world, do no more than subsidize its upkeep, it is not constructed to cope with vast numbers: there are no tea rooms, shops or visitor centres here, just two very enthusiastic and hardworking retired Englishmen, but for whose endeavours this plantsman's paradise would not exist.

Right: The woodland garden came into being in the 1920s and many of the rhododendrons were grown from seed; it contains some of the most tender and rare examples in Britain.

Right: The origins of the garden lie in the lower ground between the woodland and the hotel, containing a fascinating variety of unusual and colourful plants.

ARDUAINE GARDENS are open 1 April to 31 September, Saturday to Wednesday, 10 a.m.–6.00 p.m.

Location: on A816 Oban to Lochgilphead Road, near Kilmelford. Shares an entrance with Loch Melfort Hotel.

Left: Winding along the craggy cliff-path between azaleas and bluebells.

Crarae

INVERARAY, STRATHCLYDE

Owner: The Crarae Gardens Charitable Trust

Above: Along the banks of the burn, as it heads towards Loch Fyne, blue Himalayan poppies grow, together with every imaginable type of specie and hybrid rhododendron.

Opposite: The colourful blooms of rhododendrons and azaleas are reflected in deep pools, and the sound of waterfalls is never far away.

Down to the western shore of Loch Fyne, that long sea loch that separates Kintyre from the rest of mainland Scotland, runs a fierce mountain burn which has carved out a steep-sided glen that now forms the spine of a most remarkable garden, Crarae.

'Garden', however, is too tame a word for this almost fairytale valley, where the white of the first snowdrops, a welcome relief after a long winter, is followed by drifts of daffodils along the burn; in May bluebells carpet the woodland, acting as a perfect foil to the first azaleas, and they in turn lead into the full colourful splendour of rhododendrons and the russets, reds, yellows and golds of autumn – a changing display that is accompanied always by the thunder of the waterfalls. The magical quality of Crarae throughout the year must strike a chord in the soul of all but the most hardened of visitors.

A century ago, however, this was just a highland glen, part of the grounds of an estate owned by Sir Archibald Campbell, the great-great-great-grandfather of the present laird, Sir Ilay Campbell. Sir Archibald's predecessor, Crawford Tait, planted many Scots pine and larch in the early nineteenth century, many of which are still standing today, forming a stately backdrop to the valley. Little else, however, was planted until this century, when Sir Ilay's grandmother discovered that rhododendrons grew well in the locality and, being an aunt of Reginald Farrer, the great explorer and plant collector, she began to

introduce some of the interesting and unusual specimens which can be seen here today. Her husband, another Sir Archibald Campbell, handed the garden to his son, Sir George, in 1925, and it is from that time that the garden we see today really began to take shape.

Most of the planting until then had been around the house. The glen itself was still wild and clothed with birch, hazel, oak and alder, the only topsoil being acidic and generally shallow, overlying rock and boulder clay. Sir George, however, made the most of the pockets of peat, where he found that rhododendrons flourished, and planted such unusual species as *Rhododendron barbatum*, *R. rubiginosum*, *R. augustinii*, *R. vaseyi*, *R. fargesii*, *R. euchaites*, *R. yunnanense* and *R. sinogrande*. These and the azaleas make a significant contribution to the garden, but Crarae was never intended to be exclusively a rhododendron garden; indeed, one of Sir George's passions was the collection of rare and unusual conifers, such as *Saxegothaea conspicua* (Prince Albert's yew) from South America, *Pinus koraiensis* from Korea, and *Abies koreana* and *Cunninghamia lanceolata*. Many plants were grown from seed, while some were gifts from the owners of other Scottish gardens, such as Mairi Sawyer from Inverewe, Sir John Stirling Maxwell of Pollok and the Campbell families of Stonefield and Arduaine. Some of the unusual plants probably dating from this period include *Hydrangea integerrima*, an evergreen climbing hydrangea from Chile, *Trochodendron aralioides*, a small tree with ivy-like foliage, the Chilean shrub *Gevuina avellana* and *Philocladus trichomanoides*, a tender tree which orginated in New Zealand, but which thrives here in the lee of the house.

Sir George did not plant with any overall design in mind; each time he had a new group of plants to position he would simply clear another area of the natural scrub. It cannot be denied, however, that he had an eye for a good position, and the knowledge and foresight required for skilful grouping, planting far enough apart to allow for growth but not so far as to allow the plants to appear unrelated to

Right: The large-leaved rhododendrons and the collection of unusual conifers are a great attraction of this garden.

Right: Winding paths take the visitor high above the glen, where unusual varieties of sorbus, eucalyptus, malus, magnolia and pittosporum can be found.

Opposite: Crarae House and Loch Fyne from the glen.

each other or their surroundings. The result, as he no doubt intended over fifty years ago, is a naturalistic landscape of the type beloved by the Romantics, wild and yet slightly surreal, exotic specimens appearing to spring up quite spontaneously among familiar natives like the Scots pine.

Entrance to the garden is at the bottom of the glen, where the old vegetable and flower gardens lay. This area is at present being developed to prolong the overall flowering season and to give the elderly and disabled a flavour of Crarae without having to climb the steep paths beyond. More shrub roses are

being planted alongside flowering shrubs such as potentilla, berried shrubs such as cotoneaster and a whole range of bulbs. From here the view of the house, the lower part of the glen and the silhouette of the mountains behind whets the appetite of the adventurous, and forms an impressive backdrop to the lower garden for those who do not wish to venture further.

At the mouth of the valley one is surrounded by the dramatically contrasting foliage of *Rhododendron sinogrande*, *Ginkgo biloba*, *Gunnera manicata*, with its huge rhubarb-like leaves, and a Chusan palm, for this is no ordinary highland glen. The path winds ever higher, under a canopy of oak, beech, birch, rowan, Scots pine and larch, with a burn tumbling beside it from one rock-enclosed pool to the next. Groups of *Acer palmatum* mingle with different varieties of nothofagus, cotoneaster, berberis and azalea, contrasting and yet seeming to belong together. In autumn, the reds and yellows of the acers reflected in the deep pools enhance the magic of the climb up the steep valley, the views changing with every yard; a waterfall below is crossed by a timber footbridge, and glimpses of Loch Fyne and the mountains can be seen at intervals through the leaves. The positioning of some of the shrubs, such as *Disanthus cercidifolius*, with its cascading scarlet autumn foliage mirroring the movement of the waterfall next to it, is nothing short of inspired, as is the placing of the unusual Chinese *Hydrangea aspera* by the footbridge at the top of the glen. This top section is also spectacular in May and June, when the dazzling array of rhododendrons are in their full glory. One area has been devoted to hybrids, a majority of which are crosses made in the 1950s by the late Lord Glenkinglas at Strone on the opposite side of Loch Fyne. Two clones here were named after him, 'Secretary of State' when he was Secretary of State for Scotland, and 'Shadow Secretary' when he was in the Shadow Cabinet.

Apart from the rhododendrons, which are kept carefully in check to prevent them swamping other precious plants, some twenty

Above: Ranks of
Meconopsis sheldonii at the
bottom of the valley.

Right: Further up the path
the glen opens out to
reveal the mountains
beyond.

species of eucalyptus and numerous varieties of eucryphia, magnolia, malus, pittosporum, cercidiphyllum, styrax, sorbus, and Himalayan blue poppy in massed plantings, are all to be found in the woodland, either alongside the burn itself or by the circular ridge path which forms an alternative route back to the lower garden.

Although apparently a wild garden, the work involved in its upkeep is intensive. Steep banks make the use of machinery impractical, and chemicals are used only on paths. The head gardener, Jim McKirdy, his wife, an under-gardener, and some casual and Manpower Services Commission labour, are kept very busy removing brambles, ferns, bracken and other weeds, cutting out dead wood, thinning, removing stool shoots and so on – all very expensive, labour-intensive operations. In the years before his death in 1967 Sir George had gradually handed over the upkeep and development of the garden to his son, Sir Ilay, who in 1978 gave it to Crarae Gardens Charitable Trust – a private charity, of which he and Lady Campbell are two of the trustees – with the object of maintaining and improving the gardens for the benefit of future generations. Funds are still, however, insufficient to meet expenses, and an appeal has been launched to help pursue these objectives. In order for the garden to survive, £15,000 needs to be collected every year to establish an endowment fund, and to this end visitors are encouraged to become Friends of Crarae in return for an annual membership.

As the increase in visitors attests, there can be no doubt that at any time of the year an afternoon spent exploring the glen of Crarae will be sure to leave you firmly in its spell. Let us hope that the formation of the trust by Sir Ilay Campbell will keep the magic intact.

CRARAE GLEN GARDEN is open throughout the year, 9.00 a.m. – 6.00 p.m. (during daylight hours in winter)

Location: 10 miles south of Inveraray, on the A84 Lochgilphead road, just past Furnace.

Achamore House

ISLE OF GIGHA, STRATHCLYDE

Owner: Mr D. W. M. Landale

Gigha, meaning 'Isle of God' in Gaelic, is a favoured island in many respects: six miles long and one and a half miles wide, it has a rich, loamy, if rather acid soil, which supports good pastureland. It is also one of the most beautiful of the Inner Hebridean islands, and its silence is broken only by the distant surge of the tide on its white sandy beaches.

In the lee of the island's only major topographical feature, a small, jagged hill, lie the gardens of Achamore House, nestling on the landward side and therefore partially protected from the often fierce prevailing southwesterly winds. The air is soft, clear and unpolluted, and relatively mild, thanks to the benign influence of the Gulf Stream which means that snow is unheard of, although occasional frosts can cause damage. Rainfall is moderate but fairly evenly distributed throughout the year.

When Sir James Horlick moved to Achamore House in 1944 he decided that the climate on Gigha would be perfect for growing rhododendrons, which had not done well at his former home, Titness Park in Berkshire, and over the following twenty-eight years, until his death in 1972, he set about creating the conditions that would ensure their survival. The result is the most extensive collection of rhododendrons to be found anywhere in Scotland, and perhaps in Great Britain. Sir James was keen on plant breeding and succeeded in producing several fine crosses of his own, such as *Rhododendron* 'Gigha Gem', with a pinkish-red flower, *R.* 'Little Paddocks' (crossed in 1931), *R.* 'Titness Park', with a blood-red flower, and *R.* 'Titness Triumph', pink with a darker pink throat.

Achamore is not just significant for its rhododendrons, however. The old mixed woodland which surrounded the house, consisting largely of sycamore, beech, ash and pine, was planted at the beginning of this century, largely for pheasant cover, but was augmented by Sir James with conifers such as Sitka Spruce and other evergreens for year-round shelter. Perhaps the most startling of these additions was *Griselinia lucida*, which also lines the main driveway, and is now between three and five metres in height. *Cupressocyparis leylandii*, *Rhododendron ponticum* and various olearias and escallonias were also planted for shelter purposes; they too have thrived, and now serve visually to subdivide the woodland garden.

The traditional Scottish baronial-style house was finished in 1884 to a design by the Glasgow architect John Honeyman, and stands at the head of the main driveway overlooking a fine lawn, a wide open space at the centre of this fifty-acre garden. In a large shrub border dominated by a splendid specimen of native Scots pine (*Pinus sylvestris*) grow colourful swathes of *Erica carnea* in variety, daboecias and species of calluna, alongside the grey foliage of *Santolina chamaecyparissus* and the more colourful *Ribes atrosanguineum*. Between the house and the ridge of high land which juts upwards behind it lies the walled garden, built about the same time as the house and originally used for growing fresh fruit and vegetables for the laird's household. Today it contains some of the more ornamental plants in the garden. Next to it are the gardener's toolsheds, where you may find Malcolm McNeil, who has been carefully tending the gardens since 1958 and remembers with affection its founding years, under Sir James Horlick. In those days there were almost a dozen gardeners but today, with spiralling costs and overheads, there are only two employed full-time, although Malcolm

McNeil has part-time help from one or two students and a gardener who attends just to the vegetables. Although garden machinery and, to a lesser extent, chemicals, have improved efficiency, there are still many operations in a woodland garden such as this which can only be carried out by hand. In order to help defray costs, the present owner has established a commercial nursery since he bought the estate from Sir James Horlick in 1973, which now specializes in growing and selling those plants for which Gigha is renowned, namely rhododendrons, azaleas and camellias; the manager, Mr Hall, oversees both the garden and the nursery operations.

A path up to the viewpoint behind the walled garden leads across the Spring Bank planted with azaleas, acacias, enkianthus – with white or pink bell-flowers – olearias such as *O. nummulariifolia* and *O. chathamica*, nothofagus species from nearby Crarae, exotic-looking Chusan palms (*Trachycarpus fortunei*), cabbage palms (*Cordyline australis*), and New Zealand flax (*Phormium tenax*). The contrasting lack of vegetation on the other side of the ridge, looking over to the west side of the island, underlines the vital necessity of maintaining shelter around gardens such as this in order to ensure their continued survival. In early spring snowdrops and daffodils catch the full morning sun on this east-facing bank. It is interesting to note that the bulbs on Gigha are several weeks in advance of those on the mainland on account of the milder climate. Inside the walled garden medium-sized shrubs such as *Berberis darwinii*, *Mahonia aquifolium*, *Mahonia* 'Charity', *Senecio laxifolius* and *Abutilon vitifolium* 'Album' have grown into huge tree-like specimens, far larger than normal. There are some beautiful camellias such as cv. 'Leonard Messel' and a very rare variety of *Abies delavayi forrestii* from the Himalayas, brought to the garden by the plant collector Kingdon-Ward. This has upward-pointing spiky leaves with dark green faces and almost white undersides. Other unusual trees include *Pinus montezumae*, also from Mexico, with beautiful foliage; two *Pinus leucodermis*, from

the garden at Crarae; two *Juniperus recurva coxii*, with drooping foliage and red peeling bark; and the New Zealand Christmas tree (*Metrosideros lucida*), so-called because of the time at which it flowers. Karume azaleas, dwarf rhododendrons and herbaceous plants too numerous to mention also grow in profusion around the perimeter walls and in the central beds. There is now even a kiwi-fruit bush rambling happily over the gateway to the garden. Although it has never borne fruit, Mr McNeil has recently planted a female bush nearby in the hope that romance will blossom.

But it is the woodland garden for which Achamore is famous, and justly so. Although there is no doubt that Sir James originally intended to do no more than amass a major

Left: The sheltering function of a hedge is particularly apt here where, as well as dividing the woodland garden visually, it surrounds the 'hospital garden'.

Left: A clump of variegated hostas, with *Rodgersia aesculifolia* behind.

Opposite: One of the woodland glades displays wonderful contrasts in the shapes and textures of the foliage.

plant collection, the device of leaving glades linked by a system of paths and rides creates interest in what would otherwise be continuous woodland. Most of these glades still bear the names which he originally gave them, such as the Theatre and the Triangle. *Rhododendron barbatum* hybrids, brilliant red in flower, and *R*. 'R.W.Rye', with canary-yellow flowers and attractive red peeling bark, give way to a grove of unusual trees. The centrepiece of this area is *Betula japonica* var. 'Mandshurica', with peeling bark and tassel-like catkins, but the limelight is shared by the white-barked *Betula jacquemontii*, the rare pinnate-leaved *Sorbus harrowiana* and the pink-flowered *Prunus yedoensis*. At shrub level *Phormium tenax* and bamboo lend an exotic touch, and clumps of *Libertia grandiflora*, displaying large white flowers, grow in profusion. Unfortunately, these sometimes fall prey to rabbits, which invade the gardens despite the rabbit fence. Honeyfungus is another problem, and an extremely difficult one to eradicate.

Another glade nearby is named the Malcolm Allan Garden, after a previous head gardener. Here can be found a large *Pieris formosa forrestii*, with its flame-tipped foliage, and the more unusual *Pieris taiwanensis*, the lily-of-the-valley shrub, so-called after its white, hanging clusters of bell-like flowers, alongside *Camellia* 'Inspiration' and *C*. 'Barbara Hillier', both of which are smothered in pink flowers during May. Here too is the Chilean holly (*Desfontainea spinosa*) with yellow and red flowers, which betray the fact that it is not a true holly, and rhododendrons such as *R*. 'Brocade', with pinkish-white flowers and unusual upward-facing leaves.

South Drive, a grassy ride which once served as the main approach to the house, is now lined with rhododendrons and especially camellias: next to the family dog graveyard is the drooping foliaged *Camellia* 'F.C. Coates', or Fishtail Camellia. Two local rhododendron crosses – *R*. 'Argyll' and *R*. 'Gigha Gem' – are also worth looking out for, as is the Tasmanian waratah tree (*Telopea truncata*), which is similar to the nearby embothrium but with a mauve-coloured flower.

The central feature of the woodland garden is the pond. Occasional storm damage occurs here despite the shelter-belt, and not long ago some trees were blown down in a particularly ferocious storm, leaving a glade in which Sir James decided to create a pond. Here, white and pink candelabra primulas from Asia lead into drifts of iris, lilies, astilbes and other aquatics, with the dramatic foliage of hostas, gunnera and skunk-cabbage, with banks of rhododendrons in the background.

Sir James's concern for plants is well demonstrated by the hospital garden, enclosed by a clipped leylandii hedge, as it was here that ailing plants were put into 'intensive care'. Judging by the size of some of the rhododendrons the treatment was very successful. For example, one *Rhododendron sinograde* hybrid has leaves one and half feet long and beautiful waxy cream flower clusters; nearby can be found the statuesque *R. macabeanum*, *R. eximium*, *R. falconeri* and *R. hodgsonii*, all species with large leaves and beautiful flowers, and probably just about the best specimens of their type in Britain.

A local story tells how a visitor arrived on Gigha in the heyday of the garden and enquired of a local crofter as to the whereabouts of Sir James Horlick. Initially the man looked puzzled. He frowned and shook his head, then his brow cleared suddenly as the penny dropped. 'Ah!' he cried, 'you mean Jimmy-the-Bushes!' Doubtless Sir James Horlick will always be remembered, not only locally but nationally, for his all-consuming interest; it resulted in one of the most important plant collections in the British Isles, which draws over five thousand visitors to Gigha every year from all over the world.

ACHAMORE HOUSE GARDENS are open daily from 1 April–31 October, 8.00 a.m.–9.00 p.m.

Location: By ferry from Tayinloan, on A83 Campeltown road. Peak season: April–June.

Above: As a keen rhododendron breeder Sir James Horlick produced several fine crosses, such as *Rhododendron* 'Gigha Gem' and *R*. 'Titness Triumph'.

Left: *Gunnera manicata* forms a sculptural background to the colourful candelabra primulas beside the pond.

Above: The 'hospital garden' is enclosed by a clipped leylandii hedge. Sick plants used to be nurtured there, but now it contains healthy specimens of *Rhododendron sinogrande, R. eximium, R. falconeri* and *R. hodgsonii.*

Geilston House

CARDROSS, STRATHCLYDE

Owners: Miss Elizabeth Hendry and Miss Margaret Bell

Above: The giant wellingtonia is the central feature of the walled garden.

Elizabeth Hendry and Margaret Bell have both in their time represented Dunbartonshire at golf, with handicaps to put many other contestants to shame. They have both been County Commissioners for the Girl Guides, Miss Hendry for Dunbartonshire and Miss Bell for Glasgow, and they continue to be actively involved in the local movement (there were guides camping on their land on the occasion of my visit).

However, it is their interest in gardening which offers the most tangible evidence of their joint endeavours. Overlooking the broad reaches of the Clyde estuary in Dunbartonshire, the garden of Geilston House in many ways embodies the true character and spirit of the small Scottish garden. Although the L-shaped house dates from 1537, a keystone in the old potting shed is inscribed '1797', and it was probably then that the stone-walled garden was constructed.

Miss Hendry has lived at Geilston since 1910. Her father, a Glasgow merchant, bought the house from the Geils family in 1925. The garden was then typically Victorian in character, with large areas of bedding plants in what is now the central lawn and herbaceous perennials round the perimeter, a nightmare to maintain and rather fussy in style. Margaret Bell, the daugher of Sir Thomas Bell, one time Managing Director of John Browns, the famous Clydebank shipbuilders, had been a friend of Elizabeth Hendry since 1927, and moved to Geilston House eighteen years ago;

combining their considerable horticultural skills, they have created the very beautiful garden that we see today.

It is small by Scottish standards, the walled garden and vegetable gardens amounting to nine acres together, but Miss Hendry and Miss Bell have used every inch to maximum advantage. In common with many gardens north of the border, Geilston draws heavily on evergreens, conifers and plants with interesting barks and stems, and where possible winter-flowering shrubs, to carry it through an otherwise long and leafless winter. Although Geilston does not benefit from the Gulf Stream, the proximity of the Clyde estuary means that it is considerably milder here than inland. *Rhododendron loderii*, Exbury and Knaphill hybrid rhododendrons – seedlings from Lord Abercromby's estate in North Wales and from Crathes Castle near Aberdeen – and an array of azaleas and dwarf rhododendrons too numerous to mention, form an all-year-round backcloth to the walled garden and the picturesque glen beyond. They are also of course responsible for a dazzling display of colour from April through to August, to which *Pieris formosa forrestii*, which thrives here, adds its fiery foliage.

Cold, dry winds from the east and northeast are a perennial problem in Scotland, withering the most well-established plants, especially in eastern and central areas. Walled gardens are common throughout the country for this very reason. As rhododendrons and azaleas do not grow as well in the east, more reliance is placed in general on conifers and heathers to provide winter interest. Geilston, however, has the best of both worlds. Apart from its superb display of rhododendrons and azaleas, a striking bank of heather greets the visitor to the walled garden. Miss Bell, who is something of a heather expert, has collected about ninety different varieties in the past eighteen years. Her favourites, understandably, are the yellow- and bronze-foliaged lings and heaths, which brighten this corner all the year round; as a bonus, some also flower in late winter/early spring, when most gardens are at

their least inspiring. Two weeping *Acer palmatum* 'Dissectum Atropurpureum' complete this attractive planting scheme.

Along one side of the garden is an old orchard, now the preserve of the Geilston hens. It is separated from the main garden by a fine beech hedge planted by Miss Hendry between the wars, which keeps its winter coat of russet leaves until the fresh green of the new season's leaves comes through in April. The colours and textures of the paperbark maple, *Acer griseum*, and the silver birch *Betula alba*, also provide winter interest here.

Frost may be damaging in some of the inland areas of Scotland (minus 25°C is not uncommon in the Cairngorms in winter), but the sea's influence prevents it from being a major problem in this part of Dunbartonshire. However, when losses do occur Miss Hendry and Miss Bell take advantage of the opportunity to try out new plants, ensuring that the garden is constantly evolving and full of interest.

Although the Scottish summer is relatively brief, the growing season at Geilston is exploited to the full, and is prolonged by the sheltering stone walls. Every section of these grey stone walls is covered with climbing roses, forsythia, clematis, quince and espalier apples; the latter are particularly striking in late April/early May when white blossom covers their branches. The bones of the garden may be provided by evergreens and conifers, but the flesh is filled out in the summer by all kinds of flowering shrubs and herbaceous plants. Miss Hendry is justifiably proud of her herbaceous border, which adjoins the major axis through the centre of the walled garden, and is filled with delphiniums, lupins, Mich-

Right: The glen garden behind the walled garden is host to hybrid rhododendrons, daffodils, crocii and bluebells.

Far right: From the glen one can catch a glimpse of the walled garden through the stone gateway.

Opposite: The bronze cherub birdbath forms the focal point of the garden's major axis; behind it the enormous *Sequoiadendron giganteum* dominates the centre of the lawn.

aelmas daisies, hostas, peonies and various poppies, including the unforgettable blue Himalayan poppy. The focal point of this axis is a bronze cherub birdbath which was bought from Fortnum and Mason's in London by Miss Hendry's father, who was also a keen gardener.

Among the more unusual trees and shrubs are a massive *Sequoiadendron giganteum*, which forms the centrepiece of the garden, lindera, especially notable for its autumn colouring, ceratostigma, actinidia and *Eucryphia × nymansensis* 'Nymansay', which is covered in white flowers in August. The parterre is bordered by low box hedges enclosing hybrid tea roses. Apart from looking attractive, these little hedges have the added advantage of preventing the leaf mulch blowing away. This mulch considerably reduces the weeding in the borders, and is a useful by-product of the autumn leaf fall.

Although Miss Hendry and Miss Bell spend as much time in the garden as possible, they have a gardener, Donald Calder, who makes sure the shrub beds are kept in trim and that the lawn is as immaculate as a bowling green. A handyman, who looks after the glen below the walled garden, is also an expert at repairing walls and bridges. He has to be, as freak floods occur with frightening ferocity here – difficult to believe when the spring sun is gently filtering through the trees in the dell onto carpets of daffodils, crocii and bluebells, which bloom in profusion by the waterfalls. This dell is a small example of the Scottish glen garden, perhaps the most famous of which is Crarae in Argyllshire. Rhododendrons have almost become naturalized under the trees, bringing colour in May and June, and in autumn the trees which overhang them form a colourful backdrop to the whole garden.

Geilston House is a tribute to two remarkable ladies who have between them devoted a lifetime to creating a garden for all seasons. But it also illustrates on a small scale all that can be achieved in a Scottish garden, regardless of size, with careful forethought, a lot of perseverance and more than a little inspiration. If the perfection of Geilston House gardens is anything to go by, it would seem foolhardy to challenge Elizabeth Hendry and Margaret Bell to a round of golf.

GEILSTON HOUSE GARDENS are usually open on the last Saturday in May (or as advertised) 2.00 p.m. – 5.30 p.m.

Location: Off A814 just outside Cardross.

Finlaystone House

LANGBANK, STRATHCLYDE

Owner: Mr G. MacMillan

Above: The castellated yew hedges of the formal garden are separated from the looming hills of Dunbartonshire by the blue of the Clyde.

Though described by a sixteenth-century visitor as having many pleasant avenues with numerous plantings of various trees, the gardens at Finlaystone that we see today are mainly the product of three generations. The house, parts of which date from the fourteenth century, was extended and modernized, together with the gardens, at the turn of this century. Today it is the home of Lady MacMillan and her son George, and he, with his wife Jane, actually runs and manages the estate and the gardens, helped by his brother and sister. Each member of the family is aware of the day-to-day costs involved in running such a property, and various measures have been taken to help support it economically.

The garden has been run commercially since 1958, but it was in 1974 that the decision was taken to open up the wooded areas of the estate, to form nature trails, a fitness circuit and a picnic area, to turn the old laundry into a tea room, to further develop the walled kitchen garden as a nursery, and to open the beautiful formal gardens on the west side of the house to the public gaze. The commercial aspect, however, is kept very low-key, and on a visit to Finlaystone the most striking impression of the house and grounds is that of a lived-in and living home. The personal touch does make extensive demands on all the family in terms of time and effort, but it is one essential way of keeping costs down. Whereas at the turn of the century the estate employed fourteen gardeners, numerous foresters and a

Left: A giant stone urn
decorated with gargoyles
stands at the top of the
flight of steps which
separates the balustraded
main terrace leading to
the house from the old
carriage drive below.

Right: Part of the woodland garden contains a wide selection of unusual hybrid rhododendrons and azaleas – a blaze of colour in May.

Opposite: Azaleas and weeping cherries combine against a backdrop of a waterfall and the old laundry building to produce a Chinese willow pattern.

gamekeeper, today it has only one gardener, a countryside ranger, an estate handyman and a trainee. Lady MacMillan and her daughter Judy Hutton take an active role in garden maintenance, and in selling plants and garden requisites; Jane MacMillan and her husband George can often be seen selling tickets, promoting exhibitions of Celtic art and so on, and doing general estate work; and Lady MacMillan's other son, David MacMillan, farms the fields and sells pick-your-own fruit

Below: Seen from this angle the house is naturally framed by the rust-coloured leaves of a maple.

in the summer. Running the estate is thus very much an intensive family affair, which itself creates the informal, personal atmosphere that pervades the whole garden and adds considerably to its attraction. It has probably also paid dividends in that the number of visitors increases annually.

The garden itself can be split into four sections: wild, semi-wild, semi-formal and formal. By far the largest in terms of acreage is the wild section – mixed woodland mostly, with thickets of *Rhododendron ponticum*, which are currently being reduced in size, with more attractive and varied cultivars along the main drive. A burn runs from a pool beside the wood, past the old laundry and the New Garden, and under an elegant stone-balustraded bridge which carries the main drive; it then tumbles dramatically down two waterfalls towards the Clyde. These falls are at their most breathtaking between February and March, especially when they freeze into icicles and convoluted shapes like abstract sculpture, surrounded by bright banks of snowdrops. In April the edges of the wood are awash with the vivid yellow of daffodils, and in May a sheen of bluebells extends beneath the trees. Well documented woodland and nature rambles of varying length lead to distant corners of the estate, identifying the trees, wild flowers and the wildlife which the keen-eyed observer may see on the route. It is the countryside ranger's job to provide information on the flora and fauna of the woodlands, and guided walks are organized throughout the year. For the less energetic, there is a picnic area, and a barbeque in a clearing by an old mink farm, and for the really athletic, the fitness circuit.

The New Garden, on the edge of the woodland, appears at first glance to be semi-wild, but closer inspection reveals that it is anything but. It offers the first taste of the splendours in store: driving or walking over the bridge which crosses the burn, one is suddenly confronted by a scene straight from a Chinese willow-pattern plate. Against the backdrop of a waterfall and the picturesque

gable of the old laundry winds a slow-moving stream, with a delightful blend of carefully chosen plants on either side. These have been lovingly collected by Lady MacMillan over the years, and they range from hostas by the stream to azaleas, which look especially striking in May and June, higher up the slope; together with weeping cherries, they enhance the slightly oriental feel of this charming garden within a garden.

Also on the edge of the woodland is the great lime avenue, which originally led right down to the edge of the Clyde, until it was truncated in the last century by the coach road and then the railway. However, it is probably more majestic today: the mighty limes, like the piers of a great cathedral, frame the Clyde and the distant hills beyond.

The walled kitchen garden, which used to be further down the hill, now stands at the top, overlooking the house, and contains the well-stocked nursery. Here, Lady MacMillan and her daughter delight in helping visitors select plants for their gardens. Almost all the plants for sale here are grown *in situ* or grown-on from other British nurseries; they are consequently well-suited to the Scottish climate and have been well cared for. The walls support numerous espalier apples, which are especially attractive in May. The wrought-iron gates in the north-west corner lead to the *pièce de résistance* of the whole estate – the formal gardens on the west side of the house – and terminate the garden's main cross axis.

It is from these gates, especially on a sunny day, that the importance of Finlaystone's setting becomes immediately apparent. The fresh green of the lawns, so neatly manicured, meets the blue of the Clyde above the stone balustrade which bounds the gravel terrace, the view, in effect, becoming part of the garden rather than a mere backdrop. The castellated clipped yew hedges – like the rest of this garden – were planted in about 1900, and they enclose a central area laid out with bedding plants and a stone flower tub as a centrepiece. Although formal gardens did exist in this area before the turn of the

century, it was Lady MacMillan's grandfather who commissioned a Mr Goldring, a landscape gardener from Glasgow, to develop and extend them. A major feature of this central area is a sweeping flight of steps which leads up from the old carriage drive, flanked by a giant stone urn decorated with gargoyles. Up the hill are masses of daffodils, ilex and rhododendrons, which are especially attractive in the early summer, overhung by magnificent copper beeches. Another important feature is the huge yew, which stands on the site where John Knox is said to have given communion to the fifth Earl of Glencairn, a great supporter of the Reformation, in 1556. When the garden was extended in 1900, it was moved to its present position at the express wish of Miss Kidston, on the grounds that it restricted light into the house to such an extent that she could no longer sew!

Perhaps the most original aspect of the extended formal gardens was the use of a fold in the land to create a *trompe l'oeil* effect. The gardens end at a meadow just below this fold, but from the house the formal lawns seem to extend as far as the eye can see. Following the path round and back to the ridge of high ground above the formal gardens, the visitor moves into the realms of the semi-formal garden. Here, rhododendron and azalea varieties form the core of a blend of shrubs to which Lady MacMillan and her family have added over the years – lonicera, genista, laburnum, escallonia, forsythia, berberis and euonymus, overhung by beautiful flowering apples and cherries. The paths are chemically weeded, and beds packed as tightly as possible to reduce labour costs. A bog garden and pond have been developed in this area and may eventually form another garden within a garden. The Celtic garden is a new feature, with paving laid in the intricate form of a Celtic design from the *Book of Kells* as its centrepiece.

Finlaystone has had its moments of crisis, such as in the Second World War when two bombs fell on the garden, narrowly missing the house, and the hurricane of 1968, when seventy acres of woodland were decimated. It

Above: The Celtic garden where the paving is laid out in a pattern taken from the *Book of Kells*.

Left: A range of water-loving and marginal plants thrive around the pond at the centre of the recently developed bog garden.

has also had its share of famous visitors: Princess Mary the Princess Royal stayed here in 1964, and Mad Mitch, the late General Sir Gordon MacMillan's one-time aide, arrived for dinner one evening by helicopter. Periodically, the house and grounds are the venue for the MacMillan Clan Gathering. Add to this the usual round of visits by local schools and organizations, entertaining and exhibitions, and it becomes clear that the MacMillans are fully occupied in running the place. But what of the future? No doubt the do-it-yourself family involvement will continue to maintain the nature and atmosphere of Finlaystone very much as it is at present, and the MacMillans will develop it in the same spontaneous fashion that has recently produced the bog garden, the Celtic garden and a scented garden, to be stocked with fragrant plants. It is zeal such as this that has extended a small formal parterre into a garden of the richness and diversity of Finlaystone today.

FINLAYSTONE GARDENS are open Mondays to Saturdays, 9.00 a.m.–12.30 p.m. and 1.30 p.m.–5.00 p.m.; Sundays 2.00 p.m.–5.00 p.m.

Location: On A8 west of Langbank.
Peak Season: April–June.

Carnell House

HURLFORD, STRATHCLYDE

Owners: Mr and Mrs J. R. Findlay and Mrs J. B. Findlay

Above: An ornate gateway leads from the walled garden into the herbaceous garden, where the crisply-edged, velvet-smooth lawn slides into the shallow pool.

In 1910 Carnell's herbaceous garden was a small limestone quarry. Today it is one of the most perfect examples of its kind to be found anywhere in Scotland. Though the property lies in the agriculturally rich rolling hillsides of Ayrshire, in the heart of Burns country, it has heavy rainfall and prevailing south-westerly winds to contend with, and they can often succeed in battering down in a day an effect that has taken all year to create.

Mrs J.B.Findlay now lives in the Garden House, overlooking the old walled garden of Carnell. Today, only one side of the garden – a small proportion of the total area – is used for growing fruit and vegetables, the rest being grassed for ease of maintenance. On the opposite side, the walls give way to a cast-iron railing, and an ornate gateway in the centre leads down a flight of steps to the lower level where the herbaceous garden lies.

It was Mrs Findlay's mother who began the herbaceous garden in Edwardian times, creating the central feature of the garden, the long pool which is fed by water from the drainage pipes of the fields which lie behind it. It was after a lull of some decades that the garden was further developed: returning from service with the Royal Navy after the Second World War, Commander J.B.Findlay, R.N., enthusiastically set about the task of developing and improving the garden.

His efforts were not in vain. The herbaceous border, an especially breathtaking spectacle at the end of July, runs the full length of this linear garden from east to west, fronted by a six-foot-wide immaculately mown grass walk. South of this walk there are two major features: to the east a rock garden and to the west an oblong formal pool. Approaching the garden from the west, it is immediately apparent that the pool also marks a divide between the formal and the informal. On the left, although the herbaceous border is in itself soft and informal, its careful layering, the formality of the brick retaining wall and railings behind it, and the crisply edged velvet-smooth lawn in front, create an impression of order and discipline. The lawn seems to slide into the shallow pool whose unruffled surface reflects the summer glory of the herbaceous border. Carefully placed groups of lilies give way to drifts of campanula, astilbe and rhododendrons which spill down the bank behind and extend on peninsulas into the water. This semi-wild backdrop serves as a perfect foil for the formal perfection on the opposite bank. If the pool successfully marries the formal and informal, then its Japanese features seal the knot. Constructed between 1906 and 1914, the pagoda is contemporary with the first phase of the garden, as are the strategically placed Japanese lanterns and the teak Burmese lions, which gaze so regally down the garden from the head of the pool. These are the guardian lions or 'chinths' of Burmese temples, and were bought by Mrs Findlay's late husband on his travels in the Far East. A white timber seat of elaborate design, a locally-made copy of the original one which Mrs Findlay spotted in Ireland, acts as an eye-catcher at the end of the water, and provides an ideal spot from which to contemplate the peaceful scene ahead.

The herbaceous garden cleverly combines the natural with the disciplined in a straightforward uncluttered design. It is only about a hundred yards long but it shows just what can be achieved in a small area. As rich in colour as an artist's palette, it clearly demonstrates the degree of care with which each clump has been placed to produce the perfect gradation in height from front to back. Against the warm, south-facing brick wall, ranks of blue and

Left: At the east end of the garden a short flight of steps leads through an archway in the brick wall, marking the end of the garden.

Above: Delphiniums, scabius and *Spiraea* 'Gigantea' stand at the back of the herbaceous border which lines the south-facing brick wall, while achillea, tradescantia and phlox fill the front.

Above: A stone sundial stands at the west end of the formal pool, acting as an ornamental punctuation mark.

Right: The semi-wild backdrop of campanula, astilbe, rhododendrons and lilies, which extend on peninsulas into the pool, serve as a foil to the formal perfection of the opposite bank.

white delphiniums wave in the summer sun, some of them as much as ten feet high, carefully staked to avoid a premature end; they include the varieties 'Molly Buchanan', 'Blue Tit' and the lower 'Blue Jay'. Nearby are five-foot-high *Campanula lactiflora*, with its light purple flowers, *Sidalcea* 'Early Rose' and *S.* 'Rev. Page Roberts', with open pink flowers, and behind them lemon-white-flowered scabius which, at twelve feet, top even the ten-foot-tall *Spirea* 'Gigantea'. Towards the front, medium-sized shrubs such as *Fuchsia* 'Mrs Popple' and *Potentilla* 'Rolliston', with its strawberry-like leaves, complement the graceful clumps of red- and pink-plumed astilbes. Unusual perennials – *Gallenia trifoliata* and burning bush, *Dictamnus fraxinella* 'Alba' and the rarer purple-flowering 'Purpurea' – flourish among the more familiar evening primrose, lupins, geraniums, helenium, heuchera, and pink and purple phlox. Right at the front *Achillea ptarmica* 'The Pearl' and a purple-flowered tradescantia make perfect edging plants, while a herbaceous clematis with

small white flowers basks in the radiated heat from the sunny back wall up which it clambers.

The luxuriance of this colourful border must be due in part to the continued efforts of Arthur Allen, head gardener for twenty-two years; he is assisted by another gardener, a Youth Training Scheme employee and a part-time grass-cutter, overseen of course by Mrs Findlay's knowledgeable eye, and helped also by their secret ingredient – home-produced compost. During the war, Carnell was occupied by the army for three years, and among its tenants were officers of the Free French Army who took time off to relax in the garden. One of these officers noticed Mrs Findlay burning weeds, and suggested that she should compost the weeds instead of using artificial fertilizer. Every year since then compost has been made by alternately layering grass clippings with leaves, potato peelings, weeds and so on, and allowing air to circulate through it by a system of holes and pipes. No smell is given off, and the breakdown into friable humus is one hundred per cent successful. The Findlay family have been using organic manure now for over forty years, long before recent trends away from artificial fertilizers. In November the remains of the border are completely cut down and removed to the compost stack, and the topsoil is not forked over but simply raked. This not only saves time and labour but leaves undisturbed the bulbs of the daffodils, autumn crocii and lilies. Clumps that have grown too large are dug up and split. A layer of compost is then spread over the beds, and by the time spring arrives the goodness has returned to the soil, ready for the first thrust of new growth.

Past the herbaceous border, the pool and the Japanese pagoda, the rock garden rises steeply from the grass walk to the right. Overhung by a cypress tree until it blew down in a gale, this area, filled with all manner of interesting plants, is now flourishing. Growing like a frill round the base of a large glacial erratic boulder is *Adiantum pedatum*, an unusual relation of the maidenhair fern, with striking black stems. All types of primula, including *P. japonica* and *P. florindae* do well here, as do the ground-hugging yellow tropaeolum, pink astilbe, meconopsis and the rare Ayrshire rose, with its rose-pink flowers and small, greyish-green leaves.

A short flight of steps leads through an archway in the brick wall that terminates the vista. Nearby, adjoining the walled garden, are the greenhouse and the potting shed, which must be one of the tidiest in the country, everything neatly arranged around a picturesque fireplace, good for warming hands in the winter. In front of the Garden House Mrs Findlay has a small collection of lilies, including *L. szovitsianum* which is so happy there that it has become self-seeding.

A castellated yew walk leads back to the house. Dating from about 1500 but largely rebuilt in 1840, Carnell is now the home of Mrs Findlay's son and daughter-in-law, who are responsible for the considerable recent improvements to the borders around the main lawn. On either side of the entrance to the yew walk are azaleas, *Rhododendron* 'Elizabeth' and

geum, with *Rosa filipes* 'Kiftsgate' climbing over the walk on an archway. Elsewhere, lupins, primulas, achillea, aconitum, hostas and *Potentilla* 'Red Ace' greatly enhance the setting of the house. Facing the building, two rectangular groups of lime trees were planted to commemorate the success of the Scottish Square troop formation at the Battle of Dettingen in 1743, the two trees outside the rectangles on each side representing the officers who commanded each Square.

The high standard of maintenance also contributes to the quality of Carnell, which is a credit to all who have had a hand in developing it since the turn of the century. This little Ayrshire garden should not be missed.

CARNELL HOUSE GARDENS are open one afternoon a year at the end of July under Scotland's Gardens Scheme.

Location: Six miles from Kilmarnock, take A76 Dumfries road, turn right towards Ayr at crossroads, then two miles on the left.

Above: The Japanese lantern and a reproduction Irish seat situated at the head of the pool provide an ideal place from which to contemplate the garden.

Castle Kennedy
and Lochinch

STRANRAER,
DUMFRIES AND
GALLOWAY

*Owners: The Earl and Countess
of Stair*

Above: The Round Pond –
almost two acres in extent
– is the central feature of
the gardens.

Opposite: Looking up
from the walled garden at
the ruins of Castle
Kennedy.

From the very first moment that you swing through the gates of Castle Kennedy you are aware of the scale of these great gardens: extending to a hundred and fifty acres, they are among the largest private gardens in Scotland. The eye is drawn along a mixed avenue of beech, oak, elm, horse chestnut, larch and spruce, past a group of giant *Rhododendron barbatum* hybrids, with their deep pink flowers, and across a sparkling blue loch to the distant ruins of Old Castle Kennedy, the focal point of the main axis.

The wide stretch of water in the foreground is the Loch of Inch (known locally as the White Loch), and the higher ground on which the old castle stands is in fact a narrow isthmus, a quarter of a mile wide and a mile long, with Loch Crindil (or the Black Loch) lapping against the far shore. It is composed of glacial moraine, a mixture of sands and gravels, and the soil is therefore thin, dry and difficult to work, with any fertilizers soon washed out by the high west coast rainfall. The estate forms part of the narrow neck of land between Luce Bay to the south and Lochryan to the north which connects Stranraer and the low-lying 'Rhins of Galloway' to the higher hills of Wigtownshire behind. Although the climate is milder here than inland (with an average of less than one day's snow a year), the gardens do not benefit from the Gulf Stream to the same extent as do those of Achamore House, Arduaine and Torosay, and are very exposed to the prevailing south-westerly winds, which have frequently wreaked havoc here.

As the name suggests, Castle Kennedy was once the seat of the Kennedy family, powerful landowners in Galloway and South Ayrshire from the mid-thirteenth century. Later the land came into the hands of the Earls of Stair, renowned lawyers and statesmen. In 1716 the castle was burned to the ground and never rebuilt. It was the second Earl of Stair, a Field Marshal and British Ambassador to France, who was largely responsible for the basic layout of avenues and terracing that we see today. Inspired by the gardens at Versailles, and borrowing the manpower of the Royal Scots Greys and the Inniskilling Fusiliers – no doubt ostensibly to give them practice in building earthworks – the gardens took shape. Dettingen Avenue and Mount Marlborough, two of Castle Kennedy's early features, took their names from the Earl's campaigns. The gardens went into a decline in the early nineteenth century, but were rescued and improved by the eighth Earl who used an old plan of the original layout for guidance. Lochinch Castle was built in 1864, at the north end of the Castle Kennedy gardens, with a smaller garden laid out around it to plans by the well-known designers William Adam and Thomas Boucher.

It is the ruined Castle Kennedy, however, that holds the key to the overall layout of the gardens. It forms the hub of a giant wheel, from which axial avenues radiate like spokes in all directions, with smaller avenues running parallel or at tangents. One such axis runs due south through the old walled garden, which once supplied the castle with fruit and vegetables. From here the jagged ruins, instead of the eye-catching folly they seem to be from other viewpoints, thrust up dramatically against the sky, catching the different moods of light and weather, and offering a reminder of past greatness. Beneath the shadow of the castle, the main axis is flanked by annual and herbaceous borders containing astilbes, hostas, bergenias, hydrangeas and philipendula; elsewhere a grey border, herb garden, dwarf conifer garden and rose garden are being

gradually established. The remaining old apple trees are now bedecked by climbing roses and clematis and serve a decorative rather than practical function. By the wall nearest the castle is a sixty-foot *Grisellinia littoralis*, and two large *Eucryphia × nymansensis* 'Nyman-

say' overhang the delicate tracery of the cast-iron south gateway, which leads the eye down Dettingen Avenue and across the White Loch to the approach axis with which it is aligned.

The wide grass avenue is unusual in being lined by sturdy evergreen oaks (*Quercus ilex*), with an inner avenue of alternate embothrium and *Eucryphia glutinosa*; although damaged by the gales of 1973–4, it is still impressive. Just nearby are some fine trees which are worth a minor detour: a grove of eucalyptus which have grown to a remarkable height (some must be over a hundred feet), an unusual *Eucryphia cordifolia*, and one of the best-shaped monkey puzzles (*Araucaria araucana*) you are likely to see in Scotland. The lower branches of this species are often shed in high winds, leaving them decidedly bare below, but this spectacular specimen is well protected by surrounding trees and has luxuriant foliage almost to ground level.

Another avenue runs from the castle to the entrance gate of the gardens, where the road crosses a canal on an ornamental brick bridge. This canal is contemporary with the original layout and may have been dug for drainage purposes. The banks have recently been replanted with *Cordyline australis* which, although they tend to scorch in the more severe winters, make a statuesque entrance to the gardens. Nearby is the bowling green, established in 1733 and still in use today.

An avenue of noble fir was planted to serve as a visual link between the two castles when the new house was built; regrettably, it has become a little overgrown and no longer offers an unobstructed view, although there are plans to clear it. The main vista today is down a wide, terraced, closely mown lawn known as the Castle Green, which sweeps majestically downhill towards the Black Loch and the stepped grass mound which is named (with some imagination) the Soldier's Bonnet, another example of the second Earl's military connections. The flat area immediately in front of the castle may have originally been a parterre or heather garden, but unfortunately no record of its history remains.

Left: The monkey puzzle avenue, one of the finest and longest in the British Isles.

Left: A stone sundial dated 1896 forms the visual focus of the sunken garden beside Lochinch Castle.

Opposite: A number of visual axes converge at the ruins of Castle Kennedy, seen here from the Round Pond.

Towards the end of Castle Green a surprise awaits the visitor: to the north-west, the central feature of the gardens, the Round Pond, is suddenly revealed, and beyond it, stretching seemingly to Lochinch Castle in the distance, is the mighty monkey puzzle avenue. The Round Pond is almost two acres in extent and was originally an inlet of the White Loch. It is consequently the lowest part of the garden and the focus of adjoining avenues. When not obscured by lily pads, this still, reflective pool mirrors the rhododendron hardy hybrids which surround it on all sides. Although eighty or ninety years old, these large specimens still produce a substantial number of flowers and in some years they are absolutely outstanding, as indeed they were in 1987. Their names are unknown as many were grown from seeds brought back from the Far East by Sir Joseph Hooker and subsequently crossed many times. Some hybrids found elsewhere in the gardens, such as *Rhododendron* 'Lord Stair', *R.* 'Review Order' and *R.* 'Lochinch' do, however, offer clues to their origins. Orange- and red-flowered azaleas and *Magnolia campbellii* bloom well here too under a protective canopy of wellingtonia, *Taxodium distichum*, *Metasequoia glyptostroboides*, *Sequoia sempervirens* and *Eucalyptus gunnii*.

Planted in 1844, the monkey puzzle avenue is one of the finest and longest in the British Isles. It was hard hit by the gale of 1963, and some of the trees have been replaced, but despite suffering both salt spray drift from the west and cold dry winds from the east, it is still immensely impressive. The old pinetum, next to the avenue, also suffered grave damage in 1963. A clearing made by fallen trees has since been planted with various large-leaved hybrid and other choice rhododendrons – *R.* 'Cornish Cross', *R.* 'Penjerrick', with white flowers tinged with pink, *R.* 'R.W.Rye' (named after a previous head gardener) which has an early show of yellow flowers with red stamens, *R.* 'Review Order', possibly the best hybrid ever raised at Lochinch, and *R. vaseyi*, with pink flowers like butterflies. Another exotic specimen in this colourful glade is the

Himalayan lily *Cardiocrinum giganteum*, displaying its red-rimmed white trumpets as much as ten feet above the ground. Camellias and pieris also seem to grow quite well here, despite the thin soil. The head gardener, David Knott, uses a leaf-mould mulch to reduce weed growth and to retain moisture in the topsoil, and seems to have a fair degree of success. Owing to the size of the garden, however, he has to resort to selective and residual weedkillers in many areas.

At the end of the monkey puzzle avenue, the land drops away sharply to a meadow designed as a foil to the more formal surroundings of Lochinch Castle. The terrace in front of the castle is edged by an unusual escallonia hedge, which grows surprisingly well in this rather exposed position, overlooking the meadow and the north end of the White Loch. Other plants normally considered tender also seem to do reasonably well here, among them varieties of camellia, the white-flowered *Carpentaria californica*, *Piptanthus laburnifolius*, with yellow blossom, and on the terraced walls the blue *Clematis macropetala*. A path leads down steps flanked by ericas, callunas and Japanese maples to the Sunken Garden. This was laid out as a Victorian parterre, and its original design can still be seen in relief on the surface of the closely clipped lawn which now largely replaces the fifty-eight island beds. Only seven remain, a reflection of the dwindling workforce: three gardeners now look after the whole of Castle Kennedy and Lochinch. After the gigantic scale of the Castle Kennedy gardens, Lochinch, a picturesque garden of small-scale delights, feels intimate and almost claustrophobic. The focus is a stone sundial inscribed 1896, with a centrepiece lower down the garden formed by specimen trees such as eucryphia, cercidiphyllum and *Acer japonicum*. A variety of shrubs form a perimeter wall round the garden, among them pink rhododendron arboreum hybrids, *Pieris floribunda* and *P. taiwanensis*, *Azara microphylla* and the very tender *Eucryphia moorei*. Also found here is the largest *Pittosporum tenuifolium* in the country –

Above: Plants usually considered to be tender seem to grow reasonably well on the terrace of Lochinch Castle.

Left: The still surface of
the pond reflects the
surrounding
rhododendron hardy
hybrids – most of them
eighty or ninety years old.

fifty-two feet high: quite a feat for what is normally regarded as a medium-sized to tall shrub.

From the Black Loch more steep grass terracing leads to the lower drive, where some of the original tree rhododendrons, *Rhododendron arboreum*, can be seen arching their spectacular sprays of white flowers over the track. They are more than a hundred years old – some of the original Hooker imports – and their trunks and branches are as thick as mature trees. These are some of the finest specimens to be found anywhere in Scotland.

The nearby Giant's Grave is yet another example of the Field Marshal's 'military mounds', and affords a good view over the neighbouring Black Loch and the ancient lake dwellings, or 'crannogs' as they are called, which today look like natural islets. A small semicircular lawn to the east of the Grave, known as the Dancing Green, is backed by eucryphias and embothriums as much as forty-five feet high. There are more *Rhododendron arboreum* near this point, measuring five feet in girth and rising to over fifty feet. The Lovers' Loup footbridge finally leads back to the terraced mound next to Castle Green.

The thirteenth Earl of Stair, like his forebears, takes a personal interest in the gardens and also carries on the work of growing plants from seed. He aims to improve the facilities and attract more visitors, for, in order to survive in their present form, Castle Kennedy and Lochinch have to become economically viable. It would surely be a great loss to the nation if this survivor from Scotland's gardening history, an example of gardening with a grand vision and on a grand scale, were allowed to deteriorate and decay.

CASTLE KENNEDY and LOCHINCH GARDENS are open daily, 1 April–30 September, 10.00 a.m.–5.00 p.m.

Location: Three miles from Stranraer on A75.

Arbigland House

KIRKBEAN, DUMFRIES AND GALLOWAY

Owner: Capt. J. B. Blackett

Above: A carpet of autumn leaves in the woodland garden.

In the shadow of the rounded mountain called Criffel, on the edge of the contrasting flat expanse of the Solway Firth, lies Arbigland, one of Scotland's most southerly gardens. Tucked into a sheltering copse of beech, oak, sycamore and spruce and protected from the fierce south-westerly winds, this gem of a garden is a haven from both the weather and the outside world.

Arbigland House stands on high ground above the garden, and although it enjoys panoramic views to the north and south, its exposure to the full force of the wind makes its immediate surroundings generally unsuitable for gardening. To the north lies a small formal hedged garden, where *Primula vulgaris* and roses grow in the summer months, but the garden proper, which runs to fifteen acres, was laid out around the original house, Arbigland Hall, near the shore. Today the foundations of the building form the sunken garden, where the proximity of the sea creates a microclimate not dissimilar to that of Torquay, over four hundred miles to the south; once sheltered from the wind a surprising number of tender and unusual plants normally associated with southern England or the mediterranean can successfully be grown.

Until 1832, the Arbigland estates were owned by the Craiks, a family of great agricultural improvers who turned its 'four hundred acres of cold, unyielding clay' into productive farmland. In 1775 the new house was completed in its present form, in the Adam style,

for William Craik, the main improver of the estate. It was he who appointed, in 1730, a head gardener by the name of John Paul who was largely responsible for the layout of the gardens as we see them today. Symmetry was an important element of their design in those days, and William Craik was preoccupied with balance. On inspecting the walled garden with John Paul one day, he noticed a boy's face in the window of one of the two fruit houses which frame a distant view of the Lake District peaks across the expanse of the Solway Firth. Craik enquired what the boy was doing there and the gardener replied that he had been caught stealing fruit. To his surprise, Craik also noticed the face of John Paul's son at the window of the other fruit house, and naturally assumed that he had been caught in the act at the same time. 'Oh no, Sir,' responded the gardener, 'I just put him there for symmetry.' (The young John Paul – son of the gardener – disenchanted with a life of unpaid work living off the land, put to sea in 1761 and ended up in America, where he became a successful merchant captain. He added Jones to the end of his name after 1773 and won fame as a naval commander in the War of Independence; today he is regarded as the father of the United States Navy.)

Probably the oldest feature of the gardens is the Broad Walk: once the main carriage drive to the old Hall, today it marks the western boundary of the garden. Giant cryptomerias, sycamores, *Abies procera* 'Glauca' (the grey foliaged noble fir) and a deodar cedar are among the fine specimens lining the route, which culminates in a view of the Solway Firth and part of the rocky shore of Arbigland. Halfway along the walk is an elliptical central lawn dominated in the spring by a magnificent *Magnolia* × *soulangiana*, and nearby an unusual purple-leaved birch (*Betula pendula* 'Purpurea'). A *Rosa filipes* 'Kiftsgate', trained to climb an ancient holly, formed until recently a cascading arch of white flowers across the drive. It grew to such a size, however – over six inches in diameter near the ground – that it eventually pulled over the holly completely. It has now regrettably had to be cut back, and is only a shadow of its former self, but remains a lesson to all gardeners: never underestimate the virility of a happy plant growing in the right place.

It is hard to believe that when the present owners took over the running of the garden in 1970 it had all reverted more or less to a

Left: One of the two cherubs flanking the entrance to the sunken garden where roses and *Primula vulgaris* grow alongside the more unusual South American *Eccremocarpus scaber*.

Above: 'Japan' takes its name from the Japanese azaleas and maples which dominate this part of the garden. *Rodgersia aesculifolia* – with its unusual foliage – lends additional interest.

wilderness. It was Captain Blackett's grandmother who was the real architect of the gardens and who was also responsible for the building of the original house by the shore, in which she lived until her death in 1974. By the time her grandson and granddaughter-in-law took over the estate, she was in her mid-eighties and clearly unable to continue looking after it. It would have been tempting to abandon the gardens altogether, but bearing in mind King George VI's comment that, where nature is concerned, we are trustees for generations yet unborn, Captain and Mrs Blackett set about the daunting task of restoration and renewal. They only employ one gardener, and therefore carry out a lot of the work themselves. Although machinery such as ride-on tractors are used for grass cutting, a lot of work is still manual.

'Japan' is one of the areas they reclaimed from the undergrowth in 1974–5. Originally planted by Captain Blackett's great great uncle and aunt from the 1890s onwards, this woodland glade has been transformed by the present owners into one of the delights of the garden. A little burn bubbles out of a decorative stone spout ornamented with dolphins above a clam shell, and falls into a pool which forms the focal point of the area. *Acer palmatum* 'Dissectum' and *Acer palmatum* 'Dissectum Atropurpureum' spread their fine feathery foliage down the slope of the watercourse, and the sun shining through them casts flickering shadows on the ground, conjuring up delicate images like a Japanese painting. Another interesting maple to be found here is *Acer pseudoplatanus* 'Brilliantissimum', a small, slow-growing tree with beautiful pink foliage in the spring, which later changes to green. Shrub roses have also been planted in the dell, perhaps the most unusual being *Rosa sericea* 'Pteracantha', with its large red-winged prickles; in a damper spot grow bamboo and *Cornus florida* 'Rubra', the attractive pink-flowering dogwood from the eastern seaboard of the United States. New Zealand flax seems to grow well in this sheltered spot, and the ground is carpeted

68

Above: Autumn colours are reflected in the beech-fringed pond, once a watering hole for cattle.

Left: A short flight of steps leads down to the sunken garden, which is built on the foundations of Old Arbigland Hall.

Above: Rodgersia, hosta, candelabra primulas and acers compete to catch the eye with their interesting foliage.

with bluebells and yellow *Lamium galeobdolon* 'Variegatum', the variegated distant relative of the common nettle. Through this ground cover grows the purple-foliaged *Rodgersia aesculifolia*, which takes its name from its horse chestnut-like leaves.

An example of Captain Blackett's far-sighted approach to his garden, and of his desire to make the indentification of its plants accessible to future generations, is his novel system of numbered labelling: a key in a leaflet available at the house lists the 'Top 100 Plants', and was prepared from a survey carried out by consultants to pinpoint the most unusual and interesting plants in the garden. It avoids the problem of labels fading or going astray, sometimes falling into the pockets of light-fingered label collectors, and is a system which could be well copied to advantage in other gardens.

Facing 'Japan' is a large pond with a central island, and on the far side a stunning array of low-growing trees, shrubs and herbaceous plants border a closely mown lawn. The beech-fringed pond itself was probably originally a watering hole for cattle in the days of Arbigland Hall, but was dammed by William Craik when the catchment was increased by drainage outlets from the neighbouring fields. From the sluice, which is designed to look like an ornate stone bridge, there is another view of the Solway Firth and the mountains of Cumbria. The tranquillity of this stretch of the garden is enhanced by the sound of the waves gently lapping the shore and by the cry of seabirds.

The border around the lawn is a cornucopia of unusual and interesting plants. From the Orient come *Kolkowitzia amabilis*, the aptly-named 'Beauty Bush', *Photinia serrulata* and *P. villosa*, the former evergreen, the latter deciduous, both small trees with beautiful white spring flowers, and *Corylopsis pauci-flora*, with fine-toothed leaves and yellow flowers; from North America, *Fothergilla major*, a shrub noted for its autumn colour; from South America, *Eucryphia glutinosa*; and from Asia Minor, the Ironwood Tree, *Parrotia*

persica. Another unusual shrub is the holly-like *Itea ilicifolia*, which has long, drooping greenish-white flowers in late summer. The herbaceous border overflows with red and pink peonies, primulas, hostas, geraniums, astilbes, gladioli, lupins, periwinkles and Solomon's seal, interspersed with hydrangeas, potentilla, ribes, dogwood and dwarf species of rhododendron.

A short flight of steps leads down to the sunken garden. Enclosed by the ruined stone walls of Arbigland Hall, which rise to shoulder height in places, this is a real sun-trap, and the most sheltered part of the whole garden. The sea can be glimpsed through gaps in the overhanging oak trees, and its sound seems to be amplified by the surrounding stone walls. The regular shape of the garden has dictated its formal layout, and it has been planted with roses, ideal for such a situation, and colourful *Primula vulgaris*. Around the walls stand a number of small statues and a rich variety of flowering plants – jasmine, berberis, potentil-las, hydrangeas and tree peonies, and more unusual plants such as *Eccremocarpus scaber* from South America, *Exochorda racemosa* from China and the blue passion flower from Brazil, a tender plant which does not survive as well as this in Britain outside the home counties. A golden elm was planted in each corner of the sunken garden in 1981 to celebrate the golden wedding anniversary of Captain Blackett's parents.

Nearby is the old vegetable garden, now grassed and dissected by two paths, with a sundial dated 1815 commemorating the Battle of Waterloo at their intersection. An old potting shed, used as a studio in the summer, shares the garden with *Corylopsis platypetala*, var. Levis, a medium-sized shrub from western Szechuan in China, and *Abutilon viti-folium*, an attractive South American shrub with mauve flowers. By the walled garden, which is at the moment used only for pheasant cover (although the Blacketts would dearly like to bring it back into cultivation), stands a magnificent *Pieris japonica* over twenty feet high – one of the finest in Scotland.

Above: Bamboo, hybrid rhododendrons and conifers make unusual bedfellows in this woodland glade.

Left: The oriental atmosphere of 'Japan' is enhanced by the many different types of Japanese maple which overhang the burn.

The garden is open in the summer under Scotland's Gardens Scheme and over two and a half thousand people visit it in the course of the year. The Blacketts are keen to enable people to enjoy it even more fully, and in 1984, as part of the Dumfries and Galloway Arts Festival, the actor Edward Ballard performed a one-man play, *Old Herbaceous*, on the elliptical lawn of the Broad Walk. It told the story of an old gardener and held the audience enthralled, not just by the acting but also by the appropriate and remarkably beautiful setting.

ARBIGLAND HOUSE GARDENS are open on Sundays, Tuesdays and Thursdays, May to September inclusive, 2.00 p.m. – 6.00 p.m.

Location: Signposted from Kirkbean on the A710 Solway coast road from Dumfries. Peak seasons: May, June and September.

Central Scotland, the Borders & the East Coast

Above: Looking down across the river garden towards the River Teviot.

Previous page: Topiary at Earlshall Castle in Fife.

Peak periods: Middle to end July; early August; mid-October for autumn colour

The Central Lowlands of Scotland occupy a broad belt stretching from Glasgow in the west to Edinburgh in the east, encompassing the Forth and Clyde valleys, and bordered to the north by the Trossachs and the Ochil Hills, and to the south by the higher hills of the Borders. Both valleys are rich and fertile and generally well wooded, although the Campsie Fells to the north of Glasgow, and the Lanarkshire plateau, which lies between the two cities, are considerably higher and more open in character. The Borders have a soft mellow, pastoral quality, around the Peebles–Galashiels, Kelso–Duns area especially, where the Tweed, the Teviot and the Whiteadder rivers wind through deep, wooded valleys and rounded hills on their journeys to the North Sea. The land is generally of good quality, especially in the Duns area, which imparts a richness to the grain of the countryside and its gardens. Manderston, near Duns, combines beautiful formal gardens with landscaped parkland after the style of Capability Brown, using the natural enclosure of its Borders setting to the full; Monteviot, near Jedburgh, looks out over quiet meadows and copses beside the Teviot; and Duntreath Castle, remarkably close to Glasgow and yet in another world entirely, crouches in a picturesque valley at the foot of the Campsie Fells in Stirlingshire. Stonypath, at the southern end of the Pentland Hills in Lanarkshire, has a unique informal garden which uses its position on a high gaunt hillside as a foil for the more intimate, enclosed area around the house.

The Lowlands and the Borders share a similar type of climate. Generally a lot drier than the western coastal regions, especially towards the east, these inland areas lack the ameliorating influence of the sea. Although not as cold in winter as the north, the temperatures here can plunge dramatically and snow sometimes lies for long periods. Cold air, drainage and frost pockets can be a problem in the valleys, and east winds often arrest and shrivel new growth in the spring.

On the east coast, although the climate is slightly milder than inland, this drying wind is perhaps the main problem, coupled with the low rainfall (Tyninghame in East Lothian has less than twenty inches of rain a year), a problem aggravated by the free-draining, sandy soils. The landscape is generally open and bleak in character, with gardens of the east coast, such as Earlshall, near St Andrews in Fife, and Greywalls and Tyninghame in East Lothian, relying heavily on walled gardens and shelter planting for protection.

Although some gardens, such as Duntreath and Manderston, have collections of rhododendrons and azaleas, the gardens in central and east-central Scotland rely largely on conifers, flowering shrubs, roses, herbaceous perennials and annuals, and trees and shrubs with unusual or coloured bark, for year-round

Left: A glimpse into the formal garden at Greywalls.

interest – and sometimes a combination of all these elements, as in the magical 'secret garden' at Tyninghame. Greywalls is the only example of an Edwin Lutyens/Gertrude Jekyll design in Scotland, the style of planting in the formal walled garden scheme is informal, typical of the designs for which they are renowned. Another famous garden architect – Sir Robert Lorimer – laid out the gardens at Earlshall earlier this century on a seventeenth-century concept, with compartments formed this time not by walls but by holly and yew hedges; the sculptured topiaries here are some of the most notable in Scotland. Still more formal are the gardens of Manderston, one of the finest parterres in the country, although surprisingly once again it dates only from Edwardian times.

Rich in variety and interest, some steeped in centuries of stormy history, others more modern in origin, all these gardens are fascinating in both their content and their composition.

Duntreath Castle

BLANEFIELD, CENTRAL

Owner: Sir Archibald Edmonstone

Above: In the valley of the Blane Water, not far from Glasgow, Duntreath Castle shelters in the lee of a small, steep hill called Dumgoyach.

Opposite: An heraldic swan's head from the Edmonstone family arms surmounts one of the gateposts of the eastern gateway.

Rising like a gigantic sea wall from the gentle swell of the low hills which ring Glasgow to the north, the Campsie Fells form a clearly defined visual boundary to the valley of the Clyde, seeming to repulse the tide of suburbia which has spread so widely in other directions. For here, only ten miles from the heart of the 'Second City of the Empire', as Glasgow was once known, lies a quiet, hidden enclave, the Blane Valley, in which nestle the twin villages of Strathblane and Blanefield. As yet untouched by the spreading outskirts of Bearsden and Milngavie, which lurk only a few miles away on the far side of a low ridge, this pastoral scene is dominated at the west end by several volcanic plugs, the highest of which, Dumgoyne, can be seen from the other side of the Clyde Valley, twenty-five miles distant. In a glade by the Blane Water, in the lee of the rocky, tree-clad peak of Dumgoyach – another of these distinctive, sharply-pointed hills, though slightly humbler in scale than Dumgoyne – lies Duntreath Castle.

Coming upon Duntreath is something of a revelation. Tucked away in a tree-filled hollow, its fairytale turrets and castellations have a dream-like quality that almost makes one fear that they might fade away like some latter-day Brigadoon! The solid masonry of the old keep is reassuringly real, however. This is the oldest part of the castle and dates from 1435, when the estate was forfeited by the last Celtic Earl of Lennox and it was granted by James I to Sir William Edmonstone

of Culloden on his marriage to Princess Mary Stewart, daughter of Robert III, King of Scotland. She lies buried in Strathblane church. The castle and estate have remained in the hands of the Edmonstone family for five and a half centuries, and the present laird and his wife, Sir Archibald and Lady Edmonstone, live here permanently with their family. They have made significant alterations to the castle, notably removing all the Edwardian additions, while leaving the original keep intact.

In the gardens too they have made many changes, transforming the once neglected grounds into an appropriate setting for this romantic castle. Lady Edmonstone is currently vice-chairman of Scotland's Gardens Scheme but also serves on the gardens committee of the National Trust for Scotland and on the committee of the Historic Houses Association. Through this work she has developed a great personal interest in enriching Duntreath, a feeling shared by her husband, and their love of plants and concern to improve their garden is apparent throughout.

Approaching the castle from the north, down the main drive, one arrives first at the oldest part of the garden: the rhododendron garden lies directly ahead, to the left is the water garden, and to the right, partially hidden by a belt of conifers, is the Kings Walk. These areas were laid out in the 1920s by Sir Archibald's great aunt, the Hon. Mrs George Keppel, much admired mistress of King Edward VII, after whom the Kings Walk was named. The present laird's grandfather was a gentleman-in-waiting to the king for many years, and showed a greater interest in gardening than in the traditional pastimes of shooting and fishing. It was at about this time that Alice Keppel's daughter Violet (who was later to marry Denys Trefusis and shock society by her affair with Vita Sackville-West) described Duntreath in her autobiography as a romantic castle, quite the antithesis of the accepted image of the sombre Scottish 'ancestral pile'. Her sister, Sonia Keppel, respectable society hostess, spoke affectionately of her childhood visits to 'Uncle Archie's castle', occasions of

Above: The deeply fissured bark of a wellingtonia in the woods above the castle.

great excitement mingled with enchantment. As their horse-drawn carriage crunched through the gravel of the main driveway at the start of their holiday, they would have seen before them the mass of the old keep and the more elegant turrets of the newer additions rising majestically out of the breathtaking colours of the rhododendron garden to the north. Unfortunately, the names of the many rhododendron hybrids have been forgotten over the decades, but the sight of them is as spectacular as ever, their vivid shades blending with some very old purple-leaved plums, *Berberis thunbergii* 'Atropurpurea', and willow-leaved pears, *Pyrus salicifolia*, which give variation of colour when the rhododendrons are not in bloom.

Mrs Keppel's original water garden to the left of the driveway has been carefully restored. A lively burn falling through a series of descending pools makes an especially dramatic sight and sound in the spring months when the winter meltwater cascades from the Campsie Fells above. The edges of the pool have been completely replanted by Lady Edmonstone: among the craggy rocks are various meconopsis and primula species, including *Primula* 'Inverewe' and *P. denticulata*, which look stunning in late spring and early summer, varieties of hosta, small rhododendrons such as *R. yakuskmanum* and *R. makinoi*, hydrangea, agapanthus (which is not often seen in Scotland but seems to thrive here), *Iris purea* 'Variegata', bergenias, leucothoe, rodgersia and assorted species of variegated ground cover. There are also numerous hybrid and specie rhododendrons, recently planted behind the rocks, which should eventually provide colour in the spring and an evergreen backcloth for the rest of the year. Some of the more unusual hybrids include *Rhododendron* 'Olympic Lady', *R.* 'Peace' and *R.* 'Alison Johnstone', and some large-leaved specie rhododendrons which will look impressive in time such as *R.* 'Loderi' and *R.* rex. 'Stagshorn', sumach, *Sambucus nigra* 'Aurea', *Photinia* 'Red Robin', eucalyptus and *Magnolia wilsonii* have also been planted in this area and

are starting to knit together, and in a few years' time they will look very attractive. This water garden theme is now being continued on the right hand side of the drive, where the Kings Walk is being restored to form a woodland link with the lower garden.

The castle itself is draped with all manner of climbers, a testimony to Lady Edmonstone's love of these plants; they make an effective background to the shrubs and herbaceous plants in front and perfectly complement the grey and honey-coloured local sandstone. Among them are ceanothus, lonicera, chaenomeles, clematis, actinidia, white and blue wisteria, virginia creeper, *Hydrangea petiolaris* and all manner of climbing roses, such as the pink-flowered *Rosa* 'Albertine'. Near the castle a small chapel spans an arched gateway, which leads to the rhododendron garden and the Kings Walk, and a low stone wall semi-encloses the garden between the chapel and the keep. In front of this wall an attractive herbaceous border has been laid out and thickly planted with traditional perennial flowers in pink, white, cream and grey, with massed ranks of delphinium and aconite providing deeper blue contrasts. A raised stone rockery at the west end of this border, accented by six nineteenth-century lead cherubs, adds to the charm of this private corner of the garden. The immaculate lawn in front of the border is ideal for a game of croquet, with the air on a summer's evening heavy with the scent of roses. The nearby formal rose parterre has four beds of hybrid tea roses – 'Alec's Red', 'Doris Tyseman', 'Peace' and 'Pascali' – whose outlines are echoed by the lines of an ornamental fountain, a recent addition. This is all part of Lady Edmonstone's scheme to improve the views from the principal rooms of the castle, thereby creating 'living pictures' which change with the seasons and provide greater visual interest at all times of the year. To this end, a greater emphasis is being placed on evergreen and coniferous shrubs, as well as those with interesting bark and good autumn colour.

Two shrub borders on either side of the

chapel gateway complete the more intimate gardens around the castle itself; they are both symmetrical in their planting schemes, using a variegated weigela in each case as the centrepiece, with *Stranvaesia davidiana* 'Palette', *Kalmia augustifolia* 'Rubra', *Spiraea* 'The Bride', *Berberis thunbergii* 'Rose Glow', *Pieris formosa forrestii*, *Nandina* 'Firepower', *Cistus* 'Silver Pink' and *Viburnum davidii* all offering a good range of shape, colour and flowering periods. These shrubs are underplanted with lithospermum, dianthus, marjoram, *Sedum spectabile*, variegated mint and spring bulbs. Climbing roses, such as the pale pink 'New Dawn' and 'Morning Jewel', *Ceanothus* 'Gloire de Versailles', magnolia, assorted clematis and *Actinidia kolomikta*, with its mottled pink leaves, vigorously compete for space on the stone wall behind the shrubs and on the stone viewing turret in the corner. A matching stone turret on the other side of the castle overlooks steps, flanked by family memorials dating from 1760, which lead down to the lower part of the gardens.

The newer part of the castle dates from the middle of the last century, and faces south over a newly flagged terrace and a recently constructed flight of steps to the lower lawn. The top of the stone retaining wall which supports the terrace has just been planted with *Nepeta* 'Six Hills Giant', to form a low, weeping hedge with a cascade of blue flowers in the summer, and on either side of the steps the pink-flowered abelia from the Far East is flourishing. On the terrace itself an old millstone – the table – acts as the centrepiece of the seating area. Two stone walls have been built around it. These walls, intended partly as windbreaks, also have a decorative function; the space between their double thickness has been filled with soil that now supports a healthy growth of variegated wild strawberry, artemisia, aubretia, and various unusual alpines. Camellias seem to do surprisingly well here and add a welcome dash of pink in May.

From the terrace, the steep wooded slopes of Dumgoyach sweep down to the Blane Water running swiftly past the bottom of the garden; in the foreground the round heads of pink flowering cherries stand out in the spring

Above: Looking down from the bluebell-carpeted woods to the rhododendron garden and the chapel gateway.

Left: In front of the castle groups of cherry trees underplanted with daffodils act as a delicate foil to the backdrop of the Campsie Fells.

against a wide lawn bright with the yellow of the double form of daffodils which grow here in profusion. In the middle ground is the feature which probably adds more to the air of enchantment surrounding the castle than any other single element – the lake.

It mirrors the elegant façade of the castle and the flight of steps which lead up to it from the lower lawn, and, behind, the tree-clad lower slopes of the Campsies rising to the summit of Dumgoyne. In the gales of 1968 a stand of trees was blown down, leaving a gap at the bottom of the garden by the river, and it was decided not to replant but instead to make a lake by unblocking the water pipe which fed the old electrical generator. Today, with swans and geese gliding gracefully across its unruffled surface, it is difficult to believe it has not always been here, it seems to be so much a part of Duntreath. The image of a swan is inextricably linked with the Edmonstone family: the swan head appears in the heraldic device of the Edmonstone crest on the banner flying above the castle, and stone swans' heads flank the eastern gateway.

The area behind the lake, next to the river, has recently been planted extensively with ornamental bamboo which seems to do well in this damp, sheltered location, and round the water's edge grow *Rheum palmatum*, *Verbascum olympicum*, *Lysichitum americanum*, *Hosta* 'Albopicta', *H. sieboldiana* and various irises. It is hoped that recently planted large-leaved rhododendrons and others with unusual foliage such as *R. sinogrande*, *R. fortunei*, *R. hotei*, *R. orbiculare* and *R. williamsianum*, will enrich this area, in addition to the specimen trees such as maples, copper beech, weeping birch, cedar of Lebanon, swamp cypress and weeping elm, and groups of shrub roses, variegated hollies and weeping pears, which have been planted here in the last twenty years. A newly formed ornamental island in the middle of the lake, which can only be reached by a narrow timber footbridge, is about to be planted with species designed to add a splash of colour to this focal point of the lake. Nearby, but pre-dating the lake by about a hundred years, is a stone 'boat' with seats in the prow and stern. Its origins and purpose are uncertain, but it has been put to good use as an eye-catcher at the end of a new axis which Lady Edmonstone has created across the lower lawn.

On alternate years the gardens of Duntreath are open for a day under the Scotland's Gardens Scheme. Pipe bands play, hot-air balloons are launched, teas are served on the lawn, and a festive, fête-like atmosphere prevails. The combination of close proximity to Glasgow, unrivalled views of the Campsies and, in the distance, Ben Lomond, and the rarity of an opportunity to see the beautiful gardens, invariably put Duntreath into the top three in the gardens league in terms of total funds raised per annum, and this in a single day. When the crowds have faded away and peace returns to this romantic castle, it is not hard to see why.

DUNTREATH CASTLE GARDENS are open one day in every alternate year; the date is announced by Scotland's Gardens Scheme.

Location: On the A81 Glasgow–Aberfoyle road near Blanefield.

Right: Clever use of tropaeolum against a variegated background.

Opposite: A view of the castle and main terrace from the lake, with its picturesque bridges and central island. In the background rises the striking silhouette of Dumgoyne.

Little Sparta

DUNSYRE, STRATHCLYDE

Owner: Ian Hamilton Finlay and Sue Finlay

Above: A sundial in the sunken garden is framed by a currant bush.

On a bleak, windswept slope at the southernmost end of the Pentland Hills, near the village of Dunsyre, lies Little Sparta. The owners and creators of this remarkable garden are Sue Finlay and Ian Hamilton Finlay, who is poet first and foremost and, through the need to express himself in his surroundings, a sculptor second; he is presumably a gardener third, although he views his gardening skills merely as a vehicle for his art.

To call this a sculpture garden, as some visitors have done, is to do it a grave disservice, implying that it is no more than a sort of external art gallery; it is in fact far more than that. Western European culture has a long-established tradition of using classical features and monuments in garden design as eye-catchers and focal points, or as part of a classical or mythological theme. Indeed, the use of sculpture as part of garden design is well represented in this book. In this century, however, there has been a tendency to categorize gardens as plant collections, sculpture gardens, rock gardens and so on. One of Ian Hamilton Finlay's primary concerns at Little Sparta is to return to the classical traditions of gardening, in which garden buildings, sculpture, plants, water and landscape all have their own intrinsic value. That is not to say, however, that he does not allow compartments in the garden but each garden 'room' contains a combination of elements designed to evoke complex reactions, to stimulate social comment and provide food for

Left: In the midst of the semi-naturalized planting of the woodland garden a capital set on a plinth acts as a feature and draws the attention.

Right: This large pyramid stands in front of conifers; it is dedicated to Caspar David Friedrich, the German Romantic painter, whose work frequently included such trees.

thought, to suggest allusions to an artistic or philosophical mentor, or more simply to engender an atmosphere of peace.

Ian Hamilton Finlay came here in the late Sixties when the only tree on the site was a large ash in the south-east corner of what is now the front garden. The rest of the property was just open moorland, and it was only after five or six years of planting that it could really be referred to as a garden. It grew in piecemeal fashion from that time. There was never an overall plan; it simply evolved into its present form over a number of years, many of the artefacts around the garden being prototypes for sculptures and creative ideas that he would later develop elsewhere in Britain and Europe.

The site of Little Sparta is open and windswept, and the soil fairly thin and acidic, yet it is remarkable how well plants grow here between June and September, as if to make up

for the long, cold winter. The Finlays' single-storey stone house was originally part of a collection of farm buildings grouped around a central midden (now the temple pool); it faces south over the front garden, which consists of a number of garden rooms. In the south-west corner is the Roman garden, the first of many references to Roman and Greek mythology which, directly and indirectly, reflect Ian Hamilton Finlay's aspirations for the development of the whole garden, and his views on garden design in general. If you are expecting busts of Roman gods, you will be disappointed, however. Power in our society is represented not by omnipotent gods but by warships; tongue-in-cheek they appear here in the form of aircraft-carrier birdbaths and ornamental nuclear submarines, which, along with hostas in earthenware pots, adorn this stone-slabbed space, tightly enclosed on all sides by

Lawson's cypress. A gap in the corner opens on to a narrow brick pathway, through which grow the trunks of pine trees like weeds through a cracked pavement. A slate slab by the path is inscribed with variations on the words 'Song, Wind, Wood'. A view over a snowberry hedge shows a sweeping stretch of the valley beyond the garden, where sheep munch contentedly in open pastureland.

As the little path narrows and becomes more enclosed, three square columns mark metaphorically the journey from darkness into light. They read, in sequence, 'The contemplation of death is an obscure melancholy walk … an expiation in shadows and solitude … but it leads unto *life.*' This is adapted from a prose essay by the seventeenth-century English poet Henry Vaughan. One emerges with relief into a light, airy corner of the garden, dappled with sun under the boughs of the great ash; around the bole of the tree is a curved timber seat surrounded by foxgloves, irises and geraniums and inscribed with variations on the words 'The Sea's Waves'. Finlay's sardonic humour is visible in the grove of wild cherry trees too, a tomb-like stone bearing the epitaph 'Bring Back the Birch'.

Close by is the sunken garden, the first area to have been developed by the Finlays. It is paved with inscribed slabs and surrounded on all sides by a mass of white-flowered astrantia and ferns, with a young rowan on one side and a cherry on the other. A broad, table-like sundial stands in front of the sunken garden and growing out from beneath it is a currant bush, its bright red berries and lobed foliage forming a wreath-like frame round the dial. A grass alley, punctuated with red stepping-stones laid in a diamond pattern, leads from here to the house.

An arch laden with honeysuckle spans the path, flanked by a mass of foxgloves, dog roses, iris, currant bushes and geraniums. Behind lies a small brick-paved area where two bronze tortoises, their shells inscribed 'Panzer Leader' crawl out from underneath a potentilla. In the fruit garden nearby, even the raspberry canes, painted in random stripes of pink and green, are decorative as well as functional. The currant bushes next to them are nearly twenty years old and of considerable size.

On the opposite side of the path is the Pompeiian garden. Here, small fluted columns rise from informal groupings of campanula, spiraea, dog rose and astilbe. A central feature is a small circular pool, about two feet across, in which bobs a blue glass float from a fishing-net bearing a short inscription – 'The sphere complements the circle'; the wind ensures that the float is always changing its position.

Parallel to the front of the house is the terrace garden where *Rosa rugosa* frames inscribed slabs and monuments to lost boats and ships. The columns of the Pompeiian garden continue here, as stone capitals support a stone bench and glazed ceramic capitals act as plant pots for various types of ivy.

To the left of the front gate is a charming little enclosed area named Julie's garden after the heroine of a Romantic novel by Rousseau. Surrounded on three sides by conifers and on the fourth by the gable end of one of the garden buildings, which is smothered in an espalier cherry, it is a very private corner. A narrow brick path winds between gooseberries, apples, currant bushes, foxgloves and rowan trees, upon which hang inscribed ceramic plaques; *Lamium maculatum* (variegated dead-nettle) provides good ground cover. Past the front of the house is a giant pink cube overhung by *Sorbus intermedia* and bordered by centaurea, berberis and honeysuckle. A narrow pathway of bricks and concrete blocks laid in a basketweave pattern, and hedged on one side by spiraea, is roofed by elder and maples; this 'roof' appears to be supported by the free-standing brick piers that line the path. Tubs of Sweet William provide splashes of pink, red and mauve between the piers, alongside smaller pots containing parsley, and from an old Victorian chimney pot tumbles a variegated ivy. A side path leads to a little shrine containing a classical figure of Apollo clutching a machine-gun instead of his customary bow and arrow.

The path emerges beside the Temple of

Philemon and Baucis, which overlooks the central feature of Little Sparta – the Temple Pool. A smooth, well-manicured lawn edged with capitals, almost as if the rest of the column were buried, contrasts dramatically with the semi-wild goat willows, rowans and monkey flowers which fringe the north side of the pool. Only the white-flowered water lilies interrupt the clear reflection of the garden temple dedicated to Apollo, which fronts the pool on the west side. In front of this temple is a formal path of ceramic tiles edged with coral flower, the pink-flowering *Geranium endressii*, and a large group of iris, with their sword-like foliage. A central feature in the pond is a 'paper boat' made of marble and mounted on a column. The whole composition forms an enclosed space like a courtyard. Doves and pigeons lodge in the trees, look at the view from the rooftops or circle endlessly around the pool, their gentle cooing sounds enhancing the atmosphere of peace which pervades here.

To the north-west is the woodland garden which is full of strange and disturbing surprises. A brick path leads through the group of wild cherries, one of which has a painted white stripe up its trunk, emphasizing the fact that as objects the trees are as important and carefully placed as are the artificial elements. Nature is being used in various ways to direct our attention, or to impose a mood or feeling such as melancholy or exhilaration. Standing in a glade is another capital, this time on a stone plinth surrounded by brick paving laid in a radial pattern; the glade is enclosed by cotoneaster, elder, sycamore and more wild cherries. Inscribed slabs, broken columns behind bushes, stone seats and a sculptural relief of a mine-sweeping tank with the motto 'Hasten Slowly', make the woodland garden a place of continual discovery. On the edge of the copse, backed by a sombre planting of fir trees, is a large pyramid dedicated to the memory of Caspar David Friedrich, a German Romantic painter who included similar trees in many of his pictures.

The contrast between the dark intimacy of the woodland garden and the open hillside above is purposely dramatic and startling. The sweeping landscape with its distant hills, mostly hidden before, or seen in glimpses like pictures framed by gaps in the trees, is suddenly revealed. Here is another side of nature, the garden seems to say – open, barren, windswept, stark. A recurring theme in this area is revolution, and more specifically the French Revolution: the questions it raised then still hanging in the air unanswered. On the hillside overlooking the deceptive calm of Loch Eck lie eleven roughly-hewn stones, each weighing about a ton, as if dropped there from the heavens, with letters chiselled on them that seem to shout a message of warning over the valley below: 'THE PRESENT ORDER . . . IS THE DISORDER OF THE FUTURE.' The words are taken from a speech by the French revolutionary Saint-Just, one of Finlay's heroes. As if to echo this warning, a sinister black conning tower emerges from the blue waters at the edge of the loch; it is entitled 'Nuclear Sail', the name used for conning towers by sailors. At the far end of the loch stands a column which serves as an eye-catcher and commemorates Saint-Just.

Further up the hill is the 'Hegel Stile', a physical analogy of a philosophical concept propounded by Hegel, inscribed with the words 'THESIS: fence, ANTITHESIS: gate, SYNTHESIS: stile'. Around the Upper Pool is a small clump of alders, poplars, spruce and wild cherry, an outlier of the garden below. A plaque here dictates 'See Poussin, Hear Lorrain'. It is indeed a place for contemplation, the only sounds to disturb the silence being the bubbling of the stream and the wind sweeping across the hillside and whispering in the leaves.

An idea first explored by Ian Hamilton Finlay in his 'Sacred Grove', in the famous Kroller-Muller sculpture park in Holland, is also explored here: the base of a stone column has been fitted around the foot of each tree, turning it into a living column, each one dedicated to either a philosopher, or a theologian, scholar, artist or revolutionary who has influenced him. Robespierre, Rousseau, Carot

Above: Seeing the comment 'Bring Back the Birch' under this sycamore tree is a reminder of Ian Hamilton Finlay's sense of humour.

Above: A ceramic plaque bearing the inscription 'A.D.' hangs from the branch of a rowan tree.

Left: A large inscribed stone tablet by the upper pool suggests that the passer-by should 'See Poussin . . . Hear Lorrain'.

and Friedrich are just a few of the names from this roll of honour.

Following the little burn back down the hill, past a *Viburnum lanata* and a milestone inscribed 'Wayfaring Tree – 2 Yards', one reaches the 'Grotto of Aeneas and Dido'. A dark entrance leads into a beehive-shaped chamber, cleverly illuminated by natural light from an aperture above, which is hidden from the outside; the half-light reveals busts of the two figures who give their name to the grotto.

Ian Hamilton Finlay's poetry and three-dimensional imagery have perhaps won even more widespread acclaim abroad than in his native Scotland. But at Little Sparta the many cross-currents of his creative imagination take a unique form: here he has combined natural and artificial elements in a naturalistic setting to make something that is not only a garden but also an expression of his artistic and intellectual spirit. To a greater or lesser degree, almost all private gardens reflect their owner's inner self, and Little Sparta has become a vehicle for self-expression of a particularly creative kind. Like a good painting, it can be approached on many different levels of consciousness; every visitor can interpret it in a different way and extract as much or as little from it as they wish or perceive.

LITTLE SPARTA GARDENS are not open to the public except by appointment.

Location: near Dunsyre, Lanarkshire.

Monteviot House

JEDBURGH, BORDERS

Owner: The Marquis of Lothian

Monteviot – or Mount Teviot as it was originally known – stands, as the name suggests, on a rise above the River Teviot, overlooking the rolling Borders countryside. It is difficult to believe today that this peaceful landscape with quietly grazing cattle was once the scene of constant struggles as the Border Reivers attempted to defend their homeland against the threat of English invasion. Certainly in the garden of Monteviot there is little to remind one of the Borders' stormy history: the Marquis and Marchioness of Lothian and their son and daughter-in-law, the Earl and Countess of Ancram, are continuing the development of a garden which reflects only the relatively peaceful present.

The house itself consists of the central nucleus of a small, early eighteenth-century farmhouse to which successive generations added, creating what was in effect at one time a small village. Except for a period during the Second World War when it was used as a hospital, it has always been a private house. The oldest part of the garden still in existence is the herb garden, which is surrounded on three sides by the library and bedrooms but is open to the south, to views of the sparkling Teviot snaking its way through the meadows below. It was overlooking this peaceful setting that Jane Elliot composed the famous Scottish song-poem 'The Flowers of the Forest'. This courtyard herb garden consists of a parterre of low clipped box compartments containing almost every conceivable variety of herb. Lavender, including the tender French variety, fennel, mint, parsley, lovage, rose-

Right: Monteviot garden stands on a rise above the River Teviot, overlooking the rolling Borders countryside.

mary, tarragon and thyme grow in profusion, illustrating by their range of texture and colour their ornamental qualities as well as their culinary uses. The focal point of this attractive set-piece garden is an ornate stone sundial contemporary with this part of the house, whose stone walls surround the parterre, decked with *Rosa* 'Albertine' and the more recent *R.* 'Cecile Brunner' which has the advantage of being mildew-resistant.

Manicured grass terraces lead down towards the river to the next oldest part of the garden – the Victorian rose garden. Protected by a ten-foot-high buttressed brick retaining wall, this two-tier formal garden has supported shrub roses since it was first established. It suffered from 'rose-sickness' at one time, but the beds have recently been sterilized and replanted with groups of red and pink floribunda roses, such as 'Just Joey' which has showy peach-pink blooms. This sunny, sheltered garden has the feeling of an external room, with unrivalled views of the Teviot valley spread like a tapestry before it. The entrances, one a brick arch and the other an opening beneath an overhanging yew hedge, are to be embellished with wrought-iron gates in the near future. The top terrace has been made even more attractive by the addition of two arches over which pink rambling roses and actinidia have been trained. Blue-flowered clematis have been planted against the buttresses, and alyssum, aubretia and saxifrage tumble in profusion to the lower terrace. Seats have been placed beneath each rose arch, and to ensure that the views of the gentle Borders landscape do not become obscured in time, low-growing roses and groundcover species are to be planted in the shrub beds which the seats overlook, with higher shrubs in between, creating 'windows'.

The arboretum was probably planted at about the same time as the rose garden, in the late mid-Victorian era, when seeds were brought back to Britain from all over the world and tree collections became fashionable. The Monteviot arboretum is remarkable, however, not only for its range of species, but also in having some of the rarest and largest coniferous and deciduous trees in Britain, and indeed the world, together with various unusual crosses. Rare specimens include *Fagus sylvatica* 'Albovariegata' (variegated beech), *Quercus robur* 'Variegata' (variegated oak) – only about half a dozen other specimens of either tree exist anywhere in Britain; a Syrian juniper, the second largest in Britain and rare even in the south of England; *Quercus frainetto* (Hungarian oak) from the Balkans, and *Picea jezoensis* var. *hondoensis* (Hondo spruce) from Japan. There is also the second largest Macedonian pine in Britain here (ninety feet high) – the largest is at Stourhead; the tallest known *Acer macrophyllum* (ninety-two feet high); a very large *Larix kaempferi* (eighty-two feet high); and, until a recent gale, one of the largest beeches in Britain. The arboretum has become overgrown in recent years but Lady Ancram plans to clear the undergrowth and lay out informal paths so that these great trees can be seen to best advantage. Their towering trunks and lofty boughs give an almost cathedral-like grandeur to some of the clearings, making a walk through the already interesting arboretum an uplifting experience too.

The rest of Monteviot gardens date from 1960, when the estate came into the hands of the Marquis and Marchioness of Lothian. The house was refurbished by Edinburgh architect Schomberg Scott, grandson of the ninth Marquis of Lothian, and at the same time the river garden was planned and planted by Percy Cane, a well-known London-based landscape architect. It lies to the south-west of the house, the top end sheltered by a curved extension of the Victorian brick wall which encloses the rose garden; a turret on the wall gives a commanding view of both the river garden and the valley of the Teviot. This formal Italianate garden cleverly uses the landscape as a backdrop by leading the eye down two flights of steps to a stone 'landing stage' and thence across the Teviot to the meadows beyond. In this way, the setting becomes part of the overall design, its informality complementing the sharper lines in the foreground.

Right: The herb garden illustrates, through its range of texture and colour, the ornamental qualities of these plants, more usually grown for culinary uses.

Set into the south-facing wall at the top end of the garden is an alcove with seats looking out over the whole delightful scene.

The river garden is now being given a new lease of life by Andrew Simmons, head gardener at Monteviot since 1984, when the Earl and Countess of Ancram took over its upkeep. The borders at the top are being replanted with evergreens and rhododendrons, which will provide a background to more traditional herbaceous plants such as lilies, lychnis and agapanthus; existing island beds are being reshaped to run in a curve parallel with the back wall, and the existing shrubs, *Cotoneaster franchetii, Sedum spectabile* and *Potentilla fruticosa* have been thinned. Some of the most interesting plants, such as *Hydrangea macrondonta* and blue hibiscus, have been retained, and new shrubs such as buddleias, azaleas, and viburnum added. The south-facing walls have long been used to grow espalier apples, cherries and nectarines. Now Andrew Simmons is experimenting with plums, loganberries and blackberries, and a new cross-axis is being created to terminate the vista from the rose garden. With Andrew

Left: The herbaceous borders shelter below the brick retaining wall at the north end of the river garden. The south-facing walls have long been used to grow apples, cherries and nectarines.

Left: Part of the recently created 'red border' beside the house.

Simmons's enthusiasm and skill, and the horticultural advice of a friend of the family, Mrs Luczyc-Wyhowska, the whole garden is undergoing revitalization under the direction of Lady Ancram; it was opened to the public for one day as part of Scotland's Gardens Scheme in 1987, for the first time in six years. The Earl and Countess cannot devote as much time to it as they would like, but the improvements — both accomplished and still being planned — are surely evidence enough of their passionate interest in its continuing development.

A greenhouse has been built in which a fine array of fuchsias — 'Peppermint Stick', 'Red Petticoat', 'Eva Borg' and 'Brenda Pritchard', to name but a few — are grown for planting outside the house and for interior decoration. Here too shrub cuttings are potted-on, and tender vegetables and seedlings raised. Sweet peas, gladioli, chrysanthemums and dahlias are grown outside, mostly for house decoration, and in the nursery section shrubs are nurtured for planting out in the garden.

The area around the house has also been transformed, all-year colour being brought to a garden until recently consisting mainly of

lawns, hedges and specimen trees. *Clematis montana*, roses such as 'Kiftsgate' and newer introductions such as *R*. 'Sympathy' have been trained against the walls, and a new red border has been created, *Rosa* 'Eyepaint' contrasting with *R*. 'Evelyn Fison' and *R*. 'Europeana'. Fuchsias simmia, variegated holly, hybrid tea roses and low-growing hostas, heathers, *Ruta graveolens*, pinks, jasmine and dianthus introduce vibrant splashes of colour in the borders elsewhere round the house.

As if this were not enough, great plans are afoot for further developments. A wild garden is gradually being laid out next to the river garden, to be stocked with snowdrops and daffodils, lilies, primulas, rhododendrons and wild woodland flowers. In a clearing in the woods by the flood plain a little further on ambitious plans for a water garden, fed by an existing spring, are already taking shape, to be linked to the main garden by a footpath along the side of the meadow. The accent here will be on low maintenance, with specie rhododendrons, protected by tree belts, predominating: such tender plants would not normally grow happily in the east coast's cold, dry climate, but Andrew Simmons is confident that in this sheltered situation they will survive.

A garden is a living thing – not a museum – and at Monteviot, using a framework established over the centuries, the Earl and Countess of Ancram are developing and expanding their garden to suit their own requirements. It is an expression of their personal tastes and inclinations as well as those of previous generations. With so many large gardens in decline, it is heartening to know that this one at least is being given new vitality and that its future seems secure.

Above: A view from the top of the brick retaining wall onto the herbaceous border of the river garden below.

Right: The formal rose garden.

Opposite: The landscape of the Teviot valley beyond the rose garden plays an important part in determining the romantic character of the garden.

MONTEVIOT HOUSE GARDENS are open one day a year, normally at the end of July, under Scotland's Gardens Scheme.

Location: North of Jedburgh, turn off A68 on to B6400 to Nisbet; entrance, second turning on right.

Manderston House

DUNS, BORDERS

Owner: Mr Adrian Palmer

Above: The formal terrace is one of the few examples of its kind to be found in Scotland; it was designed earlier this century and contrasts with the Capability Brown style landscape beyond, dating from the eighteenth century.

Opposite: An unusual stone fountain on the upper terrace of the formal garden is surrounded by heart-shaped beds of red begonia, edged with alyssum and lobelia.

Everything about Manderston suggests Georgian opulence and grandeur, a garden that has matured gracefully over centuries. It is indeed one of Scotland's truly great gardens, but the astonishing fact is that nearly everything which constitutes Manderston today dates from Edwardian times.

The magnificent neo-Georgian façade of the house opens directly onto a very formal terrace, which appears at first sight to pre-date the Capability Brown style landscape which it overlooks. In fact, the lake and its parkland date from the original eighteenth-century house, and the formal terrace garden was designed earlier this century. Although the original house and grounds date from the 1790s, it was Sir James Miller, son of the eminent Victorian entrepreneur and MP for Leith, Sir William Miller, who laid the foundations of the Manderston we see today. Until then the gardens had been largely informal, consisting of the lake, formed by damming an existing burn, the Chinese-style bridge, and the pheasantry wood (later developed into the woodland garden).

Sir James married the Hon. Eveline Curzon, daughter of Lord Scarsdale of Kedleston Hall in Derbyshire, and anxious to impress his new father-in-law, he embarked on a programme of improvement on the estate, building the boathouse by the lake in 1894, the stables in 1895 and the Home Farm in 1900. On his return from the Boer War in 1901, he turned his attention to the house and gardens, and

appointed the architect John Kinross to redesign the house. When he asked about the budget, Kinross was told, 'It simply doesn't matter.' Consequently, no expense was spared, from the elaborate Adam-style interior and rich furnishings to the grandiose gilded entrance gates of the formal gardens.

At that time, the estate had a full-time staff of over a hundred; today there are only eight. One marvels at how the present owners, Mr and Mrs Adrian Palmer, who inherited the property in 1978, the head gardener and an assistant gardener, plus one helper on a Youth Training Scheme, manage to keep all fifty-six acres looking as immaculate as they must have been in Sir James's day. 'It's hard work,' admits Adrian Palmer, 'but I've tried to pull the estate into the twentieth century.' Knapsack sprayers have replaced watering cans, tractor mowers have taken over from manual ones, and the large areas of gravel in front of the house which used to take half a day to rake by hand are now done in half an hour by machine. Gone are the days when the head gardener would report to the laird for his day's duties; nowadays, working alongside the gardener, the laird prunes all the roses, trims the edges and lays out the bedding plants, while Mrs Palmer cuts all the main lawns; all this in addition to running the Home Farm. Despite the hard work, Adrian Palmer is philosophical: 'It's less a job, more a way of life,' he says, pocketing his portable telephone, another important piece of equipment on such a large estate as this. Son of the Hon. Gordon Palmer, past Chairman of Huntley and Palmers Foods, he works in the garden as often as his farming schedule permits. Although an average of 14,000 visitors per year pass through the gates of Manderston, the running costs considerably outstrip the proceeds. One reason for this is the immaculate condition in which the gardens are kept, which demands a consistently high level of maintenance.

Designed to give colour throughout the year, the gardens fall into four main sections: the formal gardens, the terraces, the lawn and lake, and the woodland garden. The terraces

were designed by Kinross at the same time as the house was rebuilt at the turn of the century, and are a perfect complement to the neo-Georgian façades. In two pools on the south terraces bronze sea creatures spout jets of water into the sky, flanked by cherubic bronze statues. Between the hedges of clipped golden yew and variegated holly, floribunda roses form a blood-red sea in the late summer,

Right: On the terrace which fronts Manderston House bronze statues are surrounded by clipped golden yew, variegated holly and blood-red floribunda roses.

Below: A walk lined by chrysanthemum leads to the grand entrance of the formal garden. The gates were gilded to reflect the glow of the setting sun.

edged by hostas. The parterre is overlooked by huge holly and monkey puzzle trees which must, by their size, date from mid-Victorian times or even earlier. Pink hydrangeas, fuchsias, potentilla, hypericum and a variety of silver-leaved plants such as *Stachys lanata* and *Lavandula spica* adorn the upper terrace.

To the east side of the house a grass terrace bounded by four large stone vases leads down, by way of an imposing gateway flanked by griffons, to two more manicured grass terraces, one used for croquet and the other for tennis. Both are overhung by a magnificent copper beech which forms a striking centrepiece. The top border, a recent addition, has been planted with hostas and pink-flowered cornelian climbing roses. A bank of rhododendrons, a riot of colour in the early summer, tumbles right down to the lake, overlooking the terraces which in turn overlook the eighteenth-century landscape, with the serpentine lake in the foreground and the woodland garden covering the facing hill. One end of the lake is bordered by some large Japanese stone lanterns and a miniature stone pagoda, surrounded by a variety of maples; their effect is especially dramatic when they are seen silhouetted against the sparkling water in the afternoon sunshine.

The woodland garden was started in the mid-1950s by Major Bailie, Adrian Palmer's grandfather, and it offers a successful contrast to the more formal areas of the garden. It is particularly remarkable for its collection of a hundred and eighty specimens of rhododendrons and azaleas. Beneath the boughs of the cryptomeria, Scots pine, larch and oak are as wide a variety of dwarf and other rhododendron as you are likely to see anywhere in Scotland – 'Yunnanense', 'Unique', 'Polar Bear', 'John Waterer's', 'Mandalay', 'Wilsonii', *R. hippophaeoides*, and many others that even eminent plantsmen would find unusual, especially on the east coast of Scotland. The variety of small and medium-sized trees is equally impressive: species with attractive bark such as *Betula jacquemontii*, *Prunus serrula* and *Acer griseum*, unusual maples such as

Acer palmatum 'Septemlobum Osakazuki' and *Acer cinnabar*, and decorative specimens such as sumac, laburnum and magnolia. Among the potentillas, berberis and large shrub roses are a few clumps of gentians which help to form the ground layer vegetation. Other features of the area include a summerhouse, a collection of stone figures and an unusual Celtic Revival-style seat known as 'the nineteenth hole'. This is probably on account of its central pillar surmounted by a pointed weather vane. The woodland garden is best viewed in early summer, when the rhododendrons and azaleas are in full bloom, and in the autumn, when the maples are a cascade of red and yellow.

To many visitors, however, Manderston's *pièce de résistance* is the formal garden, which is a joy to behold throughout the summer and early autumn. Opposite the main entrance is a wide lawn which, in the spring, is covered with daffodils, and on the other side is the grand gateway to the formal garden. At Sir James Miller's request, these gates were gilded to reflect the glow of the setting sun. They open on to a breathtaking display of colour. An elegant and unusual stone fountain at the centre is surrounded by heart-shaped beds of bright red begonias edged with contrasting alyssum and lobelia. These are bordered by massed herbaceous planting on one side and a walkway edged with chrysanthemums on the other. Straight ahead is a stone and timber pergola decked with fragrant pink climbing roses, visually separating this garden from the lower formal terrace which is flanked by stone urns and lions. It has recently been edged with 'Iceberg' roses, their white flowers a striking contrast to the yew hedge behind. The bedding plants are changed throughout the summer to ensure a constant display of colour.

Although Manderston's formal features are relatively recent additions to the eighteenth-century parkland, they were carried out with such skill that they appear to be contemporary with it, and with the Georgian style in which the house was rebuilt. Such apparent maturity is largely the result of the inspiration of Sir James Miller and his architect John Kinross,

though for the successful maintenance of their plan much credit is owed to the unceasing efforts of Mr and Mrs Palmer and their small staff to keep the estate immaculate and to retain its unique character.

Above: The timber pergola in the formal garden is smothered in pink climbing roses.

MANDERSTON HOUSE GARDENS are open Sundays and Thursdays mid-May to end of September, and May and August Bank Holiday Mondays 2.00 p.m.–5.30 p.m. Other times by appointment.

Location: Two miles east of Duns on A6105; 14 miles west of Berwick-upon-Tweed.

Tyninghame

EAST LINTON, LOTHIAN

Owner: Mr Kit Martin

Above: A huge, heart-shaped lavender bed, appearing in the foreground, and a raised stone planting bed containing *Cotinus coggygria* 'Royal Purple' are both situated in front of the herbaceous border.

Opposite: Steps leading down to the lower terrace: *Pyrus salicifolia* 'Pendula' – in the middle-ground – is one of the many silver-foliaged plants which line the upper terrace.

Tyninghame lies below the Firth of Forth on the east coast of Scotland, open to the cold, dry east winds which sweep unopposed from the Continental landmass beyond the North Sea. It was from the sea that the Vikings struck in 941, burning the little village of Tyninghame and ransacking the church of St Baldred's. A new Norman church was built on the site of the old one, and today its ruins are a striking feature of the gardens of Tyninghame as well as a tangible link with the past.

After centuries of possession by the monks of St Andrews, Tyninghame changed ownership several times before coming into the hands of Thomas, first Earl of Haddington, in 1628; the house then remained the residence of the Haddington family for three and a half centuries. In 1987, however, capital transfer tax and other estate liabilities forced the present earl to sell one of the family homes: Tyninghame was bought by Mr Kit Martin and converted into self-contained houses.

The wind of change is blowing through Tyninghame, but it is not necessarily an ill wind. The garden has evolved over many generations and some parts that we see today are less than twenty years old, despite their apparent maturity. Any future changes to the garden as a result of partition may ultimately have beneficial effects on the overall design. It is the gardens immediately around the house that will probably be affected most significantly by the new ownership. There was a house on this site long before the Haddingtons

came here, but major alterations were carried out in 1824 by the architect William Burn. The south-facing courtyard, which is enclosed by the house on the other three sides, is one feature which has changed little over the centuries. The pink stone walls are festooned with clematis and climbing roses, and around the cobbled yard clumps of senecio, lavender and cotoneaster soften an otherwise very regular space.

The courtyard faces a long terrace of pink gravel which, along with the pale pink shrub roses which line it to the south, blend with the colour of the stonework nearby. The lavender which lines the walk and other silver-foliaged trees, shrubs and perennials, such as *Pyrus salicifolia* 'Pendula', *Senecio greyi* and *Centaurea maritima*, have also been chosen to complement the stone. The person largely responsible for the skilful planting schemes around the house was Sarah, Countess of Haddington, wife of the twelfth Earl, who came to live here in 1953 and immediately set about redesigning the gardens. They had previously been based on Victorian principles, relying heavily on box parterres and bedding plants, and cared for by a small army of gardeners. Today, there are just three people to look after the whole garden, and it was this reduced labour force that Lady Haddington obviously had uppermost in her mind when replacing the bedding plants with shrubs, roses and perennials, a plan she carried out with more than a dash of flair and imagination.

Below the upper terrace is a long, low, stone retaining wall built in 1890, sheltering a deep herbaceous border which is a fine example of Lady Haddington's use of pastel colours and contrasting shapes. Over two rose cages constructed by a local blacksmith ramble salmon and blush-pink climbing roses, with yellow and white shrub roses below; vertical emphasis behind is provided by delphiniums, foxgloves and buddleia, while at the front the grey, cushion-like mounds of santolina blend with *Cotinus coggygria* 'Royal Purple'. Winter interest is provided by a few evergreens such as escallonia. The curving edge of the wide

Right: Italian statues stand at intervals along the clipped yew hedges which border the grass alley in the walled garden; the eye is led towards the Lammermuir Hills beyond.

Above: Old roses and delphiniums, dianthus, lavender and tree peonies all grow in abundance around the gazebo in the 'secret garden'.

Opposite: Pelargoniums and variegated ivy cascade from this stone urn in the 'secret garden'.

grass lawn beyond this border draws the eye to a central flight of steps leading up to a short lime avenue and the remains of St Baldred's Church. The ruins stand in a meadow where the River Tyne, East Lothian's only river (from which Tyninghame derives its name), snakes beneath mature parkland trees.

On the west side of the house, beyond the rows of pleached bay trees which line the upper terrace like a row of lollipops, is a very private garden to which the public have never been admitted. Regrettably, with the changes that may occur in the near future, they will probably never see it in its present form. This is the rose parterre, where Lady Haddington broke with her custom of using only soft blends of pastel colours, choosing instead the striking white floribunda rose 'Iceberg', the bright yellows of the hybrid tea 'King's Ransom' and the aptly-named climber 'Golden Shower'. The focal point is an unusual sundial (similar to one at Newbattle Abbey) which stands at the intersection of two paths that divide the garden into quarters. Each section is grassed and has its own centrepiece, a stone urn on a pedestal from which radiate four rosebeds surrounded by low box hedges. In the centre of each bed is a timber frame decked in roses, each quadrant alternately white and yellow, which gives a pleasing unity to the whole design.

Next to the rose parterre, but enclosed on all sides by mature trees and conifers, is the 'secret garden'. A narrow granite-setted passage roofed by lilac trees leads into a magical world where the air is still and heavy with the scent of roses: bourbon, centifolia, damask, gallica, hybrid perpetual and hybrid musk, to name but a few. They surround a white lattice-work gazebo housing a small statue, a woman with a basket of flowers representing summer. Narrow grass paths find their way through beds overflowing with blue and white delphiniums, dianthus, lavender, tree peonies, pansies, geraniums and ceanothus, beneath rose arches laden with pink and white rambling roses, honeysuckle and sweet peas. An apple alley runs through the middle of the garden, and in the spring the white

petals make a soft carpet underfoot, the boughs threading themselves through the hoops of the pergola and meeting overhead. Beyond lie the graves of two family dogs, Smoky and Ruff, with peninsular beds of *Acer palmatum*, astilbe, carpet junipers, hostas, campanula, *Rosa rugosa* and fennel. At the north end of the garden, near a neo-gothic summerhouse built in 1970, stands a little alcove containing a fountain – the gentle, hypnotic sound is the perfect accompaniment to the delights of this idyllic summer garden. Unbelievably, there was nothing here but a disused tennis court until 1965; Lady Haddington, inspired by a layout taken from an eighteenth-century French gardening book, decided to make better use of the space – a decision which visitors will undoubtedly applaud.

The landscaped parkland in which Tyninghame stands dates from the mid-eighteenth century, and part of the recent agreement of sale stipulates that this setting shall be retained in its present form, by conservation and, when necessary, replanting, *ad infinitum*. Contemporary with the parkland is a wooded area known as The Wilderness. Tyninghame was a fairly bleak location until the eighteenth century, when Thomas, sixth Earl of Haddington, decided to afforest the three-hundred-acre Muir of Tyninghame. In 1761 Thomas had published a 'Treatise on the Manner of Raising Forest Trees', in which he gives credit to the assis-

tance and encouragement of his wife. Although there is nothing left today to indicate the location of the fourteen radial woodland walks they laid out, the mighty columns of the ancient beeches remain, and the azaleas, maples and cherries planted by the twelfth earl bring splashes of colour in the spring and autumn, along with drifts of wild primroses.

Beyond the Wilderness, mellow mid-eighteenth-century brick walls enclose almost four acres of walled garden, originally the site of the minister's manse and glebe. Their previous function of growing fruit and vegetables for the main house has now been largely superseded by a more decorative purpose. The change in emphasis began in 1890, when the apple walk was planted at the south end of the garden. Until then the walls that supported vines, peaches, nectarines and espalier apples were heated internally by steam pipes; their vents, cleverly fashioned out of cast iron to look like decorative urns, can still be seen at strategic points. The apple walk takes the form of a long hooped pergola over which apple trees have been trained to form a tunnel. A box hedge 'plinth' runs the length of the walk, from which the apple 'columns' emerge, and when spring sunshine filters through the mass of white blossom, the tunnel becomes a brightly lit walk like a monastery cloister. Whenever trees have died in the past, the gaps have been immediately filled, and one hopes that the design will survive into the next century and beyond.

A stone gateway dated 1666 – a fragment of the old mansion house – leads into the main section of the walled garden. The primary axis runs roughly north-south and takes the form of a wide grass alley enclosed on both sides by an immaculately trimmed yew hedge, punctuated at regular intervals by Italian statues representing the seasons and music. The original herbaceous borders and central gravel path have, over the years, been replaced for reasons of economy by a simplified layout. The axis culminates in a series of box parterres and a specimen of the unusual *Morus alba* 'Pendula'; up a short flight of steps is a

conservatory which overlooks the walled garden, giving a spectacular view of the distant Lammermuir Hills.

The central cross axis is a narrow grass walk edged by a border of catmint, with hostas and a range of blues – buddleias, delphiniums and ceanothus – behind; overhead, carried by another hooped pergola, are the pale violet racemes of wisteria. The effect of this shimmering tunnel of violet, blue and silver is quite enchanting. Where the two axes cross, an Eros-like figure in bronze perches on a pedestal fountain which trickles water into a basin below; the space is semi-enclosed by four flat-topped clipped yews.

In three corners of the walled garden small quantities of fruit and vegetables are still grown, and parts of the old orchard remain. The fourth, however, takes the form of a miniature arboretum, started by the twelfth earl, in which specimens of eucalyptus grow surprisingly well for an east coast location. There are some unusual trees here, such as *Platanus orientalis, Cupressus amazonica* 'Glauca', *Acer circinatum* with seven-lobed curling leaves, *Acer nikoense*, which does not resemble a member of the maple family at all, and the large-leaved *Populus lasiocarpa*. In the autumn, the maples especially are a blaze of colour.

Considering the low rainfall, the hungry, sandy soils and exposed position, plants seem to thrive at Tyninghame. It is remarkable that such a superb garden has evolved here, one that holds attractions at all times of the year. We can only hope that any changes to adapt it to the new circumstances are carried out with the same skill, imagination and foresight that have been demonstrated by the Haddington family over the past three centuries.

Details of the opening times of TYNINGHAME GARDENS are not yet available, and it would be advisable to check with the house before making a visit.

Location: Near the village of Tyninghame, on the coast road to N. Berwick, A198, off the A1, east of Haddington.

Above: The central axis of the walled garden is formed by this nepeta-lined pergola.

Opposite: Bedecked by pink climbing roses, the treillage gazebo contains a statue representing summer.

Greywalls

GULLANE, LOTHIAN

Owner: Mr Giles Weaver

Above: A *Pyrus salicifolia* 'Pendula' forms the centrepiece of this side-garden between the courtyard and the holly enclosures.

Designing a house to fit into an awkwardly-shaped site of just under seven acres, between the clubhouse and the ninth green at Muirfield golf course, Gullane, was a tall order, but then Sir Edwin Lutyens was no ordinary architect. Best known, perhaps, for his designs for New Delhi, the British Embassy in Washington and the Cenotaph in Whitehall, he was also famous for his designs for English country houses and for his partnership with the celebrated Edwardian garden designer Gertrude Jekyll. The hallmark of their co-operation was the perfect integration of interior and exterior living spaces, breaking down the hard and fast barriers between the two to the point where it is sometimes difficult to define exactly where one stops and the other begins.

Greywalls was a Lutyens-Jekyll collaboration, and Miss Jekyll's brief here was not an easy one. More used to the milder climes and richer soils of the south and south-east of England, she must have regarded the prospect of adapting her ideas to the windswept eastern seaboard of Scotland as quite a challenge. Gullane, on the Firth of Forth, about fifteen miles along the coast from Edinburgh, is exposed to the assaults of wind and weather, and both golf course and garden lie on thin, acidic, greedy, sandy soils with little in the way of indigenous nutrients or humus.

The client was the Hon. Alfred Lyttleton, a keen golfer who was looking for a holiday home within 'putting distance' of his favourite golf club. How did Lutyens and Jekyll rise to the challenge of the difficult task which he had set them? Clearly they must have carried out local research, and no doubt it was Miss Jekyll who persuaded Lutyens to use walls as a central theme in the overall design, mindful of the exposed site and the successful use of walled gardens in most of the country estates of East Lothian. As a stranger to the area she undoubtedly also took note of the plants which grew well in these gardens, and at Greywalls she chose to use many more roses, which grow well here, than she had done in most of her English gardens. Lutyens was obviously keen that the house should blend with the vernacular architecture, using local 'rattlebags' stone throughout both house and garden (the name 'Greywalls' is misleading as this local stone is in fact a buff colour). The pantile capping he used for the walls and chimneys, and as a roofing material, is typical of the local style which was derived from the Franco-Dutch tradition. The design of the house may have been inspired by the battlemented ruins of Luffness Castle nearby, but equally possibly by its exposed position, which demands a building of rock-like solidity.

Certainly the designers exploited to the full the relatively small, awkwardly shaped area available to them. A small entrance garden, a little like an external foyer, presents the visitor with a conundrum. Ahead are two imposing stone gateways overhung with Scots pine, horse chestnut, Norway maple and a large white willow. Two drives — of equal width — disappear through a wall at an angle of forty-five degrees to the entrance drive, their destinations concealed. Neither do the two lodge houses, one on either side, give any clue as to which path to take. Even the planting — senecio, fuchsia and pink climbing roses — is symmetrical between the two paths. One wonders now many embarrassed visitors have ended up beside the garage in a cul-de-sac by taking the wrong fork.

The left fork leads to the house, and Lutyens here succeeded in contriving an impressive approach despite the limitations of space. Running more or less north-south, the drive

Left: Frequently framed by roses and adorned with a pattern of pantiles set in the local stone, the gateways allow tantalising glimpses into the 'garden rooms' beyond.

runs through a symmetrical open grass court-yard, its simplicity drawing attention to the rhythmic curve of the walls which completely enclose it and to the concave façade of the house, framed by two gigantic tower-like chimneys. The drive ends in a turning circle by the front door. In the curved walls are a number of doorways which allow tantalizing glimpses of colour and luxuriance, which contrast with the relative austerity of the courtyard in the same way that lush Arabic courtyards glimpsed through doorways offer an enticing contrast to the sun-baked white-washed streets. Another ingenious aspect of the courtyard is that it tricks the visitor into thinking that the gardens extend equidis-tantly in all directions, and thereby giving the false impression that the grounds of the house are twice as large as they actually are. In fact, on the west side of the courtyard, a door opens into the small garden of what used to be the gardener's cottage, the main gardens extend-

Above: Grey is the predominant colour in this part of the new herbaceous border by the holly-edged quadrants.

Below: The rose garden, a spectacular sight in the middle to late summer, lies in front of the south-east façade of the house.

ing in an easterly direction only. This cottage, now enlarged, is the home of Giles Weaver and his wife Rosamund, the present owners.

Greywalls itself was converted into a luxurious private hotel in 1948. The house had been completed in 1901, and was sold four years later to William James, who commissioned Sir Robert Lorimer to build on a new wing in the Lutyens style at the west end of the house. In 1924 it was acquired by Giles Weaver's maternal grandfather, Sir James Horlick (who also owned Achamore House, on the Isle of Gigha). When Sir James first lived at Greywalls, contrary to the original concept, flowerbeds and trees were planted in the lawns of the courtyard. Sir Edwin Lutyens, who was staying with Sir James as a guest on one occasion, was absolutely horrified by this and is quoted as saying, 'What are these flowerbeds doing, drawing the eye off the beautiful lines of my favourite house?' Needless to say, they were all removed and the area has been grassed ever since. A certain amount of colour is provided, however, by climbing roses, ceanothus, fuchsias and buddleias which grow happily up the walls without detracting from the designer's concept. An attractive detail used in the courtyard, in

common with Lutyens's work elsewhere, is the use of pantile sections to form geometric patterns in the stone wall, in this case over the gate lintels, illustrating his attention to detail as well as overall design.

Immediately opposite the opening that leads to the Weavers' house is a gateway into a side garden, which is enclosed by the semicircular wall around the courtyard and by the rear walls of the garage and stable buildings. The silvery willow-leafed pear (*Pyrus salicifolia*) makes a perfect centrepiece, with senecio, laburnum, potentilla, spiraea, weigela, and a fine example of *Garrya elliptica*, the tassel-bush, against the stone walls.

Another stone-flagged path leads back to the courtyard and directly to the front door of the main house, now the entrance to the hotel. Here Lutyens purposely confuses the definition of exterior and interior spaces, making the foyer a small-scale duplicate of the 'entrance-foyer garden'; again it offers two possible entrances but gives no clue as to which is the correct one. The use of stone flagging in this hall as well as throughout the garden serves not only a practical purpose but also an aesthetic one uniting the house with the garden rather than creating a distinct division between the two. A window seat in the gallery offers a view down the main axis of the garden, taking the eye across the formal rose beds and on to the distant Lammermuir Hills, which can be glimpsed through an elliptical opening in the garden wall. There another stone seat mirrors the one in the gallery, at the north end of the axis.

Access to the formal rose garden is once again from the courtyard in front of the main entrance. The layout of the garden is still exactly as Miss Jekyll originally planned it at the turn of the century. The central stone-flagged path is flanked by two rectangular beds which are in turn split into five by means of paths laid out in a diamond pattern. Each bed has a central standard rose, their colours ranging from white with a blush of pink to red and peach and shades of deeper pink. Around the edge and against the house are clumps of

Left: The rose garden is
laid out exactly according
to Miss Jekyll's plan of
earlier this century; in the
foreground clumps of
lavender grow from the
buff-coloured masonry
wall.

Above: One of the herbaceous borders recently replanted in the spirit of the original Jekyll design; a Scottish thistle in the foreground adds an architectural flourish.

floor to ceiling, now looks out over 'Martin's Garden', named after Giles Weaver's elder brother. Although not part of the original Jekyll garden – it was planted in 1972 by Colonel and Mrs John Weaver, Giles Weaver's parents – it remains faithful to the ideas of the original designers. The glass curtain wall and the room-like enclosure maintain the concept of the garden being integral with the house; it is lined with beds of lavender and tobacco plant, while potentilla, genista and senecio form part of the shrub border around the walls on two of the other four sides. In one corner, a eucalyptus tree is growing surprisingly well for a relatively exposed east coast situation.

An opening in a low stone wall leads from the rose garden to the central area of the main garden: here four grass quadrants enclosed by clipped holly hedges border the south-east axis from the rose garden to the garden seat and stone aperture. This central grass alley is lined by rows of *Sorbus aria* (whitebeam) and edged by two parallel mixed borders of potentilla, cotinus, peony, fuchsia, shrub roses, Himalayan poppies and globe thistles, though it is planned to replace these borders with four new beds of shade-tolerant plants. The whitebeams may also be removed as they are beginning to obscure the view of the Lammermuirs and overshadow the beds; they were not in any case part of Miss Jekyll's original planting scheme. Although the arched stone aperture and raised seat at the end of the main axis were designed to focus attention on the view of the hills, thereby making them part of the garden, a whole section of the wall – the width of the holly quadrants – was lowered by the architect to encompass a wider sweep of the East Lothian panorama. It is probable, therefore, that if more trees are to be added, they will be planted in two parallel rows leading to the outer edges of the aperture, creating a frame for the view rather than a screen across it. Another change being contemplated here is the planting of the grass quadrants with shrubs in central beds, using a different colour for each area.

Until he retired in 1987, James Walker had

blue lavender, Mexican orange blossom and pittosporum. In the middle to late summer, when the Lyttleton family – the original owners – were in residence, and when the hotel is at its busiest today, this garden is a spectacularly colourful sight. The two open-air garden rooms on either side of the rose garden have both been covered in, but again they were probably originally intended to blur the distinction between the inside and outside living areas. One, the summer house, which adjoins the main building, has been converted into a tea room, while the other, known affectionately as 'The King's Loo', is now a self-contained bedroom. Its name derives from its most famous patron – King Edward VII, who was a friend of William James, visiting Greywalls on many occasions. The 'throne' of this open-air closet was strategically positioned opposite an opening in the wall through which the outline of the Lammermuirs could be contemplated at leisure.

A gateway through the wall by the rose garden leads to what was once a tennis court. A modern one-storey extension in the style of the house, with a passageway glazed from worked as gardener and later head gardener at Greywalls for sixty years, since the era of Sir James Horlick. This has given a strong element of continuity to the gardens. The challenge to carry on the good work has been taken up by a younger man, Julian Haines, who has a full-time and a part-time gardener to assist him. One of Mr Haines's first projects has been to recreate some of Miss Jekyll's herbaceous borders along the cross axis between the rose garden and the holly-edged quadrants, and although it always takes a few years for such a border to get established it is clearly going to be a most attractive feature, especially as many of the species selected are unusual ones. At the back are anchusas, their flowers like vivid forget-me-nots carried on five-foot stems, *Angelica archangelica*, *Rheum palmatum* (the 'oriental rhubarb'), filipendula, trollius (the globe flower), macleaya (the giant plume poppy), and thalictrum (meadow rue). Towards the front are low-growing and ground-covering species: anaphalis, with its small white flowers and silver leaves, *Pulmonaria* 'Mrs Moon', with spotted leaves and bright pinkish-purple flowers, *Heuchera americana* (the aptly named coral flower), *Mimulus* 'Mrs Whitecroft' (the yellow-flowered monkey musk), often naturalized by watercourses in parts of Scotland, astrantia and *Dicentra orgenona*, with its pink, bluebell-like nodding flower heads. A variety of annuals and perennials mingle in the beds opposite, beneath standard specimens of *Sambucus racemosa* 'Plumosa Aurea', the cut-leaved golden elder, planted at ten-foot intervals.

To the east end of the garden there are plans afoot to extend the area under vegetables and herbs into the existing putting green, and greenhouses have recently been erected for growing cut flowers. A new central axis is also being established here and planted with herbaceous material, once again following the traditions of the Jekyll garden.

Finally, to the north of the main house, is the third important feature of Greywalls – the sunken garden, with its views of the tenth hole of the Muirfield golf course in the foreground and the majestic sweep of the Firth of Forth beyond, with the Forth road and rail bridges to the west, and ahead the coastline of Fife. In total contrast to the walled gardens at the back, this area is completely open, with just a ha-ha to divide it from the green in front. The close proximity of Greywalls to the course, where the Open Championship is played regularly, has attracted such internationally renowned golfers as Nicklaus, Watson, Trevino and Palmer, who have stayed here regularly over the years. Problems do exist, however: the front garden is so open and exposed that sinking it was the only practical way to provide sufficient shelter to enable plants to grow. Even so, being north-facing, it only receives sunlight for three months of the year and is essentially a summer garden; it is at its peak when the championship is held, usually in early August. It consists of a central sunken lawn surrounded by four drystone retaining walls about two feet high, in and against which hostas, hebes, geraniums, spiraea, fuchsia and helleborus grow, although they are sensible enough not to peep too high above the parapet. It is an exhilarating garden, and an excellent foil to the enclosed courtyard and the walled garden.

Elsewhere in the British Isles many Lutyens houses have survived in good repair while their Jekyll garden has been altered beyond the point of no return. In Greywalls, however, Scotland is fortunate to have, in its only surviving Lutyens/Jekyll composition, a well maintained and faithfully conserved example of their work. It shows how satisfying the result can be when architect and garden designer work in close co-operation, and subsequent owners keep their vision alive.

GREYWALLS GARDENS are open to residents and non-residents from mid-April to end of October. It is also open one day a year under Scotland's Gardens Scheme, usually at the end of June, as advertised.

Location: By Muirfield golf course, Gullane, on the Edinburgh to North Berwick road, A198.

Below: An elliptical opening above the garden seat terminating the main south axis frames the view of the Lammermuir Hills beyond.

Above: Beds of lavender and roses line the axis running south-east from the house. In the middle-ground, to the right, stands the building known as the 'King's Loo'.

Earlshall Castle

LEUCHARS, FIFE

*Owners: Major and
Mrs D. R. Baxter*

Above: A herbaceous
border beside the lawn is
known as the 'Bowling
Green', although it is
never used as such. In the
background stands a
summerhouse designed
by Lorimer.

Had it not been for an enlightened bleach merchant from Dundee, Robert Mackenzie, who bought Earlshall Castle in 1890, when it was already in an advanced state of disrepair, we might see today only the crumbling remains of another Scottish castle surrounded by a wilderness. Although his friends were convinced it was financial suicide, Robert Mackenzie had two winning cards up his sleeve: a vision of what it could look like, and an architect who could realize this vision – Robert Lorimer (later knighted), the son of his friend Professor James Lorimer.

Lorimer was not only a skilful architect but also a clever and sensitive garden designer, who was clearly attracted by the idea of making a garden that would match the spirit and character of the castle. Although the garden is less than a century old, it complements the castle so perfectly that it seems to have been there as long as the building itself. From his first inspection of the site, Lorimer was clearly enthused by Earlshall's surroundings, and was already picturing its potential: 'The natural park comes up to the walls of the house on the one side, on the other you stroll out into the garden enclosed. That is all – a house and a garden enclosed, but what a promise can such a place be made! Such surprises – little gardens within the garden, the ''month's garden'', the herb garden, the yew alley.'

The fourteen acres of parkland still extend to the front of the castle, with a herd of picturesque highland cattle held at bay only by a lupin-filled ha-ha. There are thirty-four acres of woodland too, mainly Scots pine, oak, sycamore, beech and birch, sheltering an abundance of wildlife. The Baxters have opened up nature trails, and even the Royal Air Force base at nearby Leuchars does not seem to dissuade foxes, roe deer and red and grey squirrels from making their homes there.

What has changed, however, is the 'garden enclosed': bounded by ancient walls were three and a half acres of vegetable garden, unusual in lying immediately next to the castle itself. It was the potential of this rare opportunity which Lorimer immediately, and almost instinctively, seized upon. He saw in his mind's eye a sixteenth-century garden, unaffected by the Renaissance, a garden contemporary with Earlshall itself which was built by an ancestor of the present owners, Sir William Bruce, in 1546. Although the building was carefully restored by Lorimer, it had escaped the fate of many Scottish castles and had never been substantially altered or extended since the day it was first constructed. It was its feeling of antiquity which Lorimer sought to capture in the garden he designed for it.

Between the castle wall and a two-storey building engagingly called 'Dummy Daws', after a dumb eighteenth-century coachman, lies the castle courtyard, where pink and grey cobblestones eddy around the old octagonal castle well, with its picturesque wrought-iron pulley wheel. Island troughs of geraniums and alpines spill colour on to the cobbles, an old rosemary bush sprays a fountain of blue flowers in a corner, and orange blossom and honeysuckle soak up the warmth against the stone wall of the castle. Like stepping-stones through a whorl of cross-currents, a flagged path winds its way through the cobbles to the topiary garden, half glimpsed between a stone balustrade and the branches of the enormous lime which overhangs the courtyard.

If Lorimer conceived his design of the garden as a series of external rooms and compartments, then the topiary garden must be seen as being the main room; physically it

Above: A stone arbour with a hood-like canopy lies at the end of the yew alley.

Left: Ranks of sweet peas brighten this corner of the kitchen garden, while the stone monkeys which adorn the roof bridge of the tool shed add interest behind.

Right: The topiary yews reputedly represent chessmen but seem more often to depict stylized birds and abstract shapes.

Far right: The Shakespeare quotation inscribed over this doorway designed by Lorimer reads, appropriately, 'Here shall ye see no enemy but winter and rough weather.'

is closest to the castle itself, and is overlooked by all the east-facing windows. The topiary yews, for which Earlshall is best known, came originally from a disused garden in Edinburgh. They were already a reasonable size when they were moved, and it is said that Lorimer promised £5 to the head gardener for every tree which survived. Much to everybody's surprise, all thirty endured the rigours of transplantation, and the £150 they earned the gardener of the day must have represented a king's ransom. The topiary yews were first clipped into shapes in the 1920s, and subsequent gardeners have kept them as close to the original designs as possible. Although they are supposed to represent chessmen, closer inspection reveals that a majority are in fact convoluted abstract shapes, and one or two are stylized birds. It is much more likely that Lorimer planted them in the form of four saltires (diagonal crosses), a design which can be fully appreciated from the upper floors of the castle. Whatever the intentions of the original and subsequent gardeners, the smoothly clipped topiary yews reflect the vertical lines of the castle and seem to have the same solid character and antiquity, which makes them inherently right for their location.

In the stone wall at the end of the topiary garden, a gateway, one of Lorimer's additions, leads into the woodland beyond; above it an inscription from Shakespeare's *As you Like it* reads, appropriately, 'Here shall ye see no enemy but winter and rough weather.' Fortunately, a lot of the rough weather which comes in from the North Sea is filtered by this extensive shelter belt and by the garden walls, and the garden itself is generally well protected from all but the strongest winter gales. Beside the gateway grows an ivy-smothered buddleia with unusual light blue panicles, alongside senecio, spiraea, pieris, broom and a large tassel-bush.

All the 'gardens within the garden' are divided by walls of clipped yew and holly so that each one is a revelation, with openings offering unexpected vistas. Running from east to west beside the topiary garden is the yew alley, just as Lorimer envisaged, terminating in a stone arbour near the gateway at the far end of the garden. On either side of the arbour the junction with the wall is marked by a slate-capped stone pillar, from which a castellated wall sweeps up and over a semicircular seat in a hood-like structure supported by black-stained timber beams. A sundial is set amidst a mass of floribunda and hybrid tea roses, many of which have won prizes in the local flower

Left: Next to the castle is the topiary garden, overhung by a huge lime which grows by the courtyard.

Right: Wired espaliers, with gnarled branches bowed low – 'heavy with shining apples' – grow amidst herbs and vegetables.

show, and the air around the arbour is filled with their heady scent.

A grass walk leads west up the yew alley, in which alcoves at regular intervals contain specimen plants such as fuchsia, *Rosa fragrantissimum* and *Azalea* 'Gibraltar'. Its destination, glimpsed through the frame of a holly arch, is the secret garden immediately behind Dummy Daws.

Lorraine Baxter describes this area fondly as a 'controlled riot'. It is certainly a riot of colour throughout the summer. Once a pond which was filled in, it is now a maze of irregular stone slabs with a path across the middle and masses of geraniums, love-in-the-mist, lewisia (a drift of pink flowers in July) and white jasmine pushing up between the stones; in a sunny corner on the wall behind, climbing hydrangea, camellia, standard roses and lamb's-ear (or, in the local vernacular, 'Lambie's lug') are all flourishing, and *Bergenia cordifolia* cleverly masks the bare stems of the clipped, castellated holly hedge which encloses the area.

An arched opening in the hedge leads to the orchard garden, which is enclosed on two sides by clipped holly and on the other two by the old walls surrounding the vegetable garden. The central feature here is a stone plinth draped in honeysuckle and surrounded by a grove of ancient apple trees, some of which still produce fruit. Colour is provided in summer in this private corner of the garden by annuals such as asters, cornflowers and marigolds, with a mixture of herbaceous perennials and shrubs along the walls, and in spring by the yellow trumpets of daffodils and the white blossom of the apple trees. It is difficult to believe that when the Baxters arrived in 1983 all that could be seen under the trees was a mass of nettles and other weeds, all of which were removed by hand.

The sheltered orchard garden leads to the relative openness of the rose terrace, which overlooks a large lawn known as the 'Bowling Green', though it has not recently been used as such and is soon to be turned into a croquet

Left: In the 'secret garden' looking eastwards it is possible to see geraniums, lewisia and white jasmine pushing up from between irregular stone slabs.

lawn. A considerable amount of work has been carried out in this area, especially since the Baxters acquired the property, to introduce a spectrum of colour to enliven the sombre yews and hollies that form the backbone of the garden. Old roses and hybrid teas line the hedge behind the terrace, and along the front weathered basins containing aubretia, saxifrage, rock campion, oxalis, achillea and penstemon alternate with stone benches – which offer a good view of the garden below. Inlaid in pebbles on the stone terrace is the 'Lynkit Heartis' (linked hearts) motif taken from the painted ceiling of the long gallery in the castle.

A short flight of steps leads down to the lawn, where a path runs parallel to the yew alley below a retaining wall; above it are two colourful herbaceous borders known as the 'High Place' and the 'Professor's Patch', the latter after Major Baxter's father. On and around the stone wall at the front are alpines and sedum, with pansies and dianthus, lavender, montbretia and peonies behind. Astilbe and *Echinops ritro*, planted at intervals along the back, provide height and punctuation, showing up particularly well against the yew hedge behind. Pink-flowered shrub roses on either side of the central flight of steps frame the view through to the topiary garden. Another herbaceous border divides the path from the lawn, and below the rose terrace is 'Queenie's Plot', containing mostly red and pink-flowering roses such as 'Iced Ginger' and 'Evelyn Fison'. Verbena, tradescantia, aster, hebes and *Potentilla* 'Miss Wilmott' have been added to give substance to the bed with little rock plants such as *Alyssum montanum* and dwarf penstemon at the front.

The shady north-facing wall beside the lawn was a challenge, but the Baxters have been successful in combining shade-tolerant specimen yews with underplanted annuals such as nasturtiums, and perennials such as aconitum, echinops and rodgersia. In one corner is an attractive summerhouse, another of Lorimer's creations, which is shortly to be renovated. The immaculate lawn was infested with moss and invaded by moles until 1985 when it was dug up and completely resown. The result is a credit to the garden and a perfect setting for the borders, with their background of yew and holly hedges and the castle rising majestically behind.

At the opposite, northern end of the topiary garden, is the kitchen garden, and once again Lorimer had very clear ideas about its layout right from the start. He wrote that the kitchen garden was, 'nothing to be ashamed of, to be smothered away from the house, but made delightful by its laying out ... on either side borders of brightest flowers backed by low espaliers hanging with shining apples, and within these espaliers the gardener has his kingdom ....' Divided from the topiary garden by a castellated holly hedge, the kitchen garden is approached along an avenue of pleached limes which runs the entire length of its east side. From the entrance this avenue looks like a long corridor, but views open up on either side, and to the right of the path are some unusual shrubs such as *Desfontainea spinosa*, with its small holly-like leaves and pendulous, reddish-yellow, tubular flowers, and *Crinodendron hookeranum*, whose red lantern-like flowers bloom in May. Both are natives of Chile and more usually found in gardens on the warmer west coast of Scotland. A very healthy camellia and a New Zealand flax also testify to the mild microclimate enjoyed by Earlshall.

Two grass walks divide the garden into four, lined by wired espaliers 'heavy with shining apples' – just as Lorimer envisaged – and edged with parsley, following his precept of combining the decorative with the practical. Inside each quadrant grow cabbages, potatoes, strawberries and, on ranks of canes, raspberries. A large herb garden, backed by a group of bay trees, also serves a dual purpose: plumes of fennel, clumps of dill, chives and borage are all within easy picking distance of the kitchen, but they are as attractive as they are useful and, as Lorimer advocated, they have not been tucked away out of sight. Most

of the James Grieve apples, pink shrub roses and tree peonies which grow here date from his original planting, and when they die the Baxters plan to replace them wherever possible with similar species to keep his original scheme alive.

In the north-east corner of the kitchen garden is the tool shed, where 'the gardener has his kingdom'. Built in 1899, this two-storey building, which has two stone monkeys gambolling on the roof ridge, was another of Lorimer's creations. The head gardener today is Henry Colliar, who has been at Earlshall since 1939; he has a young assistant, and another gardener comes to cut the grass at regular intervals.

A brick path in a herringbone pattern leads to the Dowry House, which is used for occasional exhibitions and for storing apples in the winter. Alongside it grow pink, cream and carmine roses, pink and purple pyrethrums, and beds of lilies, irises and peonies, many of them cut for flower arrangements for the castle. Finally, a path edged with Michaelmas daisies leads past more magnificent tree peonies to the courtyard, where the expedition began.

In creating a garden fit for Earlshall Castle, the young Robert Lorimer succeeded brilliantly, and were he and his enlightened client, Robert Mackenzie, still alive they would no doubt be delighted that his original concepts have been adhered to and are being conserved for future generations by the Baxter family. As a result, we can see the vision he saw of the Golden Age laid out around an authentic sixteenth-century castle in a fascinating succession of interconnecting alleys, garden rooms, lime walks and topiary.

EARLSHALL CASTLE GARDENS are open on Easter Saturday, Sunday and Monday, and thereafter from Thursday to Sunday inclusive until the last Sunday in September: 2.00 p.m.–6.00 p.m.

Location: Signposted from the village of Leuchars, A919 Dundee–St Andrews road.

Above: A wrought-iron thistle motif is incorporated into a side-door in the wall of the kitchen garden.

Opposite: Rock plants and perennials are encouraged to grow through the gaps in the stone slabs in the secret garden – a controlled riot of colour in the summer months.

The North & North-East

Above: *Lysichitum americanum* in the water garden at Kildrummy.

Previous page: A peaceful scene at Kildrummy Castle in Grampian.

Peak times: May, June, late July-early August

Perth is often referred to as the 'Gateway to the Highlands' and, indeed, from Perthshire and the River Tay northwards the landscape changes, first subtly, in the hillsides which border Crieff and the Carse of Gowrie, and then more dramatically as the Grampian mountains thrust upwards, reaching over four thousand feet in the Cairngorms.

In northern Scotland there are vast tracts of wild, uninhabited land, and consequently settlements, let alone gardens, are few and far between. It is in the agriculturally richer lowlands of Aberdeen and Angus, bordering the coast to the east and north-east, and in the hills of Perthshire, that a large proportion of the gardens of this huge area of Scotland are concentrated. Drummond, Scone, Rossie Priory and Brechin are just some of the stunning gardens that ring the approaches to the highlands: Drummond, a striking formal garden dating from the seventeenth century, is laid out in the form of a saltire, its plan only fully appreciated from the castle which stands on rising ground above it. The grounds of Scone Palace contain the best example of a private pinetum in Scotland, with towering redwoods and sitka spruces; Rossie Priory has a fine water garden surrounded by yew arches; Brechin, with a magnificent walled garden and pond, formal walks, and groves of laburnums, cherries and unusual birches, is one of Scotland's finest private gardens.

Further north are the valleys of the Dee and the Don, running from the peaks of the Cairngorms towards the North Sea, beyond the lush fields of Aberdeenshire. Royal Deeside is recognizably highland in character, the lower slopes of the Cairngorm peaks clothed in pines and fir trees, the craggy upper slopes purple with swathes of heather. At Balmoral magnificent formal herbaceous borders and rose beds, and the recently developed water garden make a spectacular contrast with the wild scenery beyond. The countryside of the Don valley is altogether more gentle and undulating, the land more fertile and less rugged. In the steep-sided valley of a tributary of the Don lie the gardens of Kildrummy Castle, overlooked by the ruins of the old castle and spanned by a bridge. The alpine garden in the old quarry and the water garden below make full use of their dramatic setting.

The climate in all these areas is not dissimilar to that of central Scotland, except that temperatures in winter drop even lower, and the winter season and the snows which it brings last a little longer, night frosts lingering in hollows into May and even June. The east wind is an ever-present problem here in springtime, as it is in the south-east, and the need for shelter is paramount. It comes as a surprise, then, to find on the road to Wick and John O'Groats, the formal gardens of Dunrobin Castle, which support relatively tender plants such as fuchsia, escallonia, olearia and

Left: Part of the stone balustrade near the main house at Rossie Priory.

arelia. Dunrobin owes its success largely to the shelter afforded by protective walls and extensive woodland planting, and its position immediately next to the sea.

Generally speaking, this is not good rhododendron country, and the gardens of north and north-east Scotland are given shape and substance by the conifers from North and South America, which also provide much-needed shelter. Roses, herbaceous borders, heathers, alpines and flowering shrubs are used to provide colour and interest from May until August, before the return of the long, cold winter. Although summer may be a brief season in the north of Scotland, her private gardens certainly make the most of it.

Drummond Castle

CRIEFF, TAYSIDE

Owner: The Grimsthorpe and Drummond Castle Trust

Above: The 'thistle parterre' is given vertical emphasis at ground level by a row of Japanese maples.

Opposite: The main axis runs through the centre of the 'saltire' motif, where it is punctuated by the seventeenth-century sundial; it then continues up the hill opposite.

Among the low, rolling hillsides and pleasant woodlands of Perthshire, near the village of Muthill, lies Drummond Castle, its sturdy keep dating back to 1491. The house, enclosing a cobbled courtyard, was begun in 1689 by James, fourth Earl of Perth and Chancellor of Scotland, and it is from this courtyard that visitors have their first impressive view of Drummond's famous gardens.

The castle itself stands on a ridge of high ground overlooking a wide level area to the south, which is enclosed on the far side by a wooded hill. Between the two ridges lies the great formal parterre. It is from the two viewing terraces at the front of the castle that the splendours of the garden can be seen as a whole, and its perfect symmetry and the placing of individual elements, can best be appreciated. It was clearly intended to be seen from above as the finer points of the layout lose their wider significance at ground level. In that respect it has something in common with Dunrobin Castle in Sutherland, but the similarities end there, and it is fair to say that Drummond is a unique garden of its type in Scotland and probably also in Great Britain.

The viewing terraces themselves, studded with white marble busts and pleached purple plums, set the tone for the formality of the parterre below. The centrepiece of the garden is an elaborate sundial, and this, together with the kitchen garden and a small part of the terrace, is all that is left of the original gardens of 1630, which were laid out by John Drum-

mond, second Earl of Perth. Like an obelisk in shape, the sundial has about fifty faces set into the stone, which tell the time in most of the capitals of the world. The first verse of an inscription on its base reads:

We are the hours on the pillar you see,
Marked by the shadows that ever flee,
And move with the sun in its course on high,
Noting the time passing swiftly by.

Four clipped purple plums surround the sundial, and the ground around its base has been paved in pebbles laid to form a mosaic of alternate black and white wavy lines, a design taken from the arms of the Drummonds.

Intersecting at the sundial are two diagonal grass walks linking opposite corners of the garden, each diagonal edged along its entire length with the little white flowers and downy, silver leaves of *Anaphalis triplinervis*, which comes originally from the Himalayan foothills. From the terrace it is clear that the walks have been laid in the form of a saltire, or St Andrew's Cross. The parterre was designed in this form in 1839 by George Kennedy, who may well have been influenced by the taste for gardening in the French style, of which there was a revival at that time.

To the east and west of the sundial that other Scottish emblem, the thistle, is described in a tracery of low box hedges infilled with buff-coloured gravel, the head of each thistle outlined in Japanese maple. A symbolic form of the thistle also appears on the slope leading down to the gardens from the castle, although on so huge a scale that it is not recognizable as such except from the south side of the garden. The purple-foliaged *Cotinus coggygria* 'Royal Purple' forms the flower, with golden juniper, potentilla and *Hypericum patulum* 'Hidcote' representing the highly stylized foliage.

It is from the bottom of the impressive double flight of steps which leads down this slope that the main axis of the garden runs. It follows a straight course, roughly north to south, through the central sundial and a stone colonnaded garden building beyond, and on

via a swathe cut through the wood to the top of the hill on the far side, where it culminates in an eye-catching statue on the skyline. The axial line is marked by a gravel walk flanked – opposite the foot of the steps – by two imposing statues: one represents a fisherman with a net and trident, the other a hunter carrying freshly killed game. On either side of the walk are two large gravel expanses of identical shape, with a radial design of low box hedging extending from each corner, infilled with pink hybrid tea roses; four large *Acer palmatum* 'Dissectum Atropurpureum' flank the path, and a statue forms the centrepiece of each symmetrical design. Like most of the statuary in the garden, these were placed here in about 1820, and the stone tubs nearby, inscribed with the Drummond arms and the family motto 'Gang Warily', date from 1840.

Equidistant from, and parallel to, the central path, on either side of the two gravel areas, are two other north-south paths which pierce the centres of the two thistle motifs. The point where each one crosses the saltire is marked by four clipped purple plums accentuating the arms of the cross. Rows of immaculately trimmed golden yews and hollies run out to the corners of the garden, clipped into cone shapes or round-topped standards. At the termination of each of these side axes on the south side of the parterre is a stone archway over which tall yew hedges form a roof.

One of the two huge copper beeches, which are such an important feature of the south end of the garden, was planted by Queen Victoria on her three-day visit to the gardens shortly after their completion in 1842. (The grandeur of the newly finished parterre and the castle behind it is captured in a contemporary painting of the scene by Jacob Thompson, depicting, rather fancifully, the royal entourage enjoying a picnic in the foreground.) In keeping with the overall design of the garden, both trees are perfectly equidistant from the central axis. The garden is enclosed to the south and west sides by a well-trimmed beech hedge, a departure from the more usual masonry or brick wall which protects so many

Above: The garden is divided by the two diagonal axes of a saltire: sandwiched between two of the arms lies a parterre of box hedging and gravel representing the Scottish thistle motif.

Above: Beds of iceberg roses and clipped yews surround one of the fountains.

Left: Looking up from the 'thistle parterre' towards the castle.

Scottish gardens from the elements. This may perhaps be because this has always been a decorative garden while many others started their lives as kitchen gardens, whose walls were important not only for shelter but also for growing espalier fruits.

At either end of the garden, to the east and west, is a shallow dish-like pool in which a central statue is bombarded on four sides by water jets. Beds of 'Iceberg' roses radiate outwards from each pool in a fan pattern, the edges punctuated by alternate dark and golden Irish yews trimmed to form columns.

The perfect symmetry of the garden is broken only by the seventeenth-century low-arched castellated stone bridge which carried the original driveway over the corner of a small pond at the east end of the garden. The pond itself does not contribute to the overall design, and the tiny portion which intrudes upon the garden is hidden by a yew hedge. A group of eighteenth-century yews of massive proportions, which balance a smaller group on the opposite side, completing the symmetrical plan, occupy the north-east corner near the bridge. The huge hummocky form of one of

the yew trunks has been hollowed out inside like a cave, enclosing a statue with a celestial globe. As well as serving a decorative function it is a good place to shelter in bad weather.

There are four gardeners at Drummond, but the work required to keep the place immaculate is endless: just one example is the cypresses at the southern end of the garden, which are all nearly thirty feet high and are trimmed into perfect cones. The standard of maintenance is generally so high that it is

Right: The viewing terrace is dominated by the presence of the castle, as indeed is the rest of the garden.

difficult to see a blade of grass, let alone a leaf, out of place.

In the mid-1970s the Grimsthorpe and Drummond Trust was established by the twenty-sixth Lord Willoughby de Eresby, third Earl of Ancaster, to finance and maintain the buildings, gardens and woodland for the benefit of future generations. His daughter, Lady Willoughby de Eresby, is now the chairman of the Trust and takes a close personal interest in the gardens, helping to ensure that this spectacular and unique parterre is maintained in pristine condition.

DRUMMOND CASTLE GARDENS are open seven days a week, 1 May–31 August; Wednesdays and Sundays during September, 2.00 p.m.–5.00 p.m., and one day a year under Scotland's Gardens Scheme.

Location: Off the Crieff to Muthill road, to the north of Muthill village, Perthshire.

Left: The white-flowered *Anaphalis triplinervis* links the four corners of the garden as it forms the arms of the cross of St Andrew. A decorative urn is one of the many prominent Italianate marble features of the design.

Right: Scone Palace, although first built in 1580, was rebuilt between 1802 and 1804, having been sacked during the Reformation.

Opposite: The first Douglas fir ever to be grown in Europe was grown at Scone – from seed sent back from Columbia in 1826 by David Douglas, who was born and raised at Scone.

knees as a penance for their sins. Alder, ash, rowan, willow and sycamore grow here in profusion, as well as some juniper and yew.

Perhaps the most well-known feature of the whole garden, however, is the pinetum. It was started in 1848, when a hundred and sixty-three conifers, all of them rare or exotic, were planted by the Earl of Mansfield. Today there are about a hundred and fifty trees representing fifty-two different species, at least five of which were originally planted in 1848. The majority have now reached maturity and the present earl has embarked on an ambitious programme of replanting among the existing trees and also in an adjacent plot. There are two main avenues in the pinetum, running roughly north-south, one of which is composed of western hemlock (*Tsuga heterophylla*), the other of noble fir (*Abies procera*). These avenues allow welcome shafts of sunlight to penetrate the twilight in the closely planted pinetum, and also serve roughly to demarcate the distribution of species. To the west, wellingtonias (*Sequoiadendron giganteum*), the tallest species of tree in the world, tower above Lawson's cypress (*Chamaecyparis lawsoniana*) and various species of fir. In the central strip are other fir and spruce varieties and to the east of the tsuga avenue monkey puzzles (*Araucaria araucana*) are mixed with fir, hemlock and chamaecyparis. Scattered around the edges are yews (*Taxus baccata*), both the common and the golden-foliaged

varieties, and various species of pine. The size of the trees is breathtaking: the four sitka spruces (*Picea sitchensis*) to the east of the hemlock avenue are the tallest in Britain, measuring 157 feet in 1981 and still growing at the rate of one foot a year! The height of the Lawson's cypress trees – some around a hundred feet high – would probably alarm the average suburban gardener. Equally impressive is the range of foliage to be found here – the pendulous spines of Brewer's weeping spruce (*Picea breweriana*), the long, radially-arranged needles of the umbrella pine (*Sciadopitys verticillata*), the spikes of the Chinese fir (*Cunninghamia lanceolata*) – and the widely different growing habits of the trees themselves, such as the convoluted Colorado white fir (*Abies concolor*) and the very erect red silver fir (*Abies amabilis*). Nurturing young conifers is not an easy job with rabbits, deer and the Scottish climate to contend with, and the head gardener, Peter Timoney, and his two groundsmen have a huge task on their hands.

On average, 104,000 visitors pass through the gates of Scone Palace every year to enjoy not only the gardens but also, in the summer months, the cricket matches, grand banquets, shooting parties and craft shows, and in the autumn a 'farming of yesteryear' display. Some have come in a more official capacity, however: Mary Queen of Scots, King James VI, the Crown Prince of Japan, the King of Sweden, and more recently Margaret Thatcher have all planted trees here. In 1983 the Queen Mother planted an oak tree grown from an acorn from the tree which King James VI had planted three centuries before, thereby strengthening the sense of historical continuity which is so much a feature of the gardens.

SCONE PALACE GARDENS are open from Good Friday until the second Monday in October, Mondays to Saturdays, 9.30 a.m.–5.00 p.m. Sundays, 1.30 p.m.–5.00 p.m.

Location: Just outside Perth on A93, Braemar road.

Rossie Priory

INCHTURE, TAYSIDE

Owners: Lord and Lady Kinnaird

Above: Gunnera manicata (giant rhubarb) overhangs a well-maintained gravel path above the water garden.

Opposite: Over the past ten years the addition of primulas, meconopsis, hosta, iris and astilbe – amongst others – has revitalised the water garden, seen here from below, looking up towards the waterfall and the weeping elm.

Rossie Priory lies on the edge of low wooded hills overlooking the wide, fertile Carse of Gowrie and the River Tay, not far from Dundee. An early Regency Gothic house, it derived its name from its cloister-like covered walkways rather than from any monastic associations.

There have been gardens of some sort at Rossie since the house was first constructed in 1807, and when the main block of the old building was pulled down in 1950 the foundations were used as the basis for a new terrace garden, which has a magnificent view of the whole valley. Stone steps flanked by twin eighteenth-century Italian cannons and more recent carpet junipers lead up to a stone pathway, which was once the main corridor of this part of the old house, and is now the 'gravel garden'; where once there were rooms there are now shrub roses and bedding plants. At the end of this path, where French windows used to open over extensive lawns and the oldest cricket ground in Scotland, lies a foundation stone eighteen feet long, twelve feet wide and six inches thick: it is impossible to imagine how this massive slab, which must weigh several tons, was moved here in the early nineteenth century from a quarry four miles away.

In front of the gravel garden is an herbaceous border, where geraniums, poppies, astilbes and hydrangeas all grow well in the fertile soil; they share it with some lime-loving plants which approve of the outwash from the

old walls which also offer protection from the cold east winds that sweep up the valley. Nearby are island beds containing several plants of interest including *Parrotia persica* (the Ironwood Tree), *Viburnum tomentosum* and *Hydrangea villosa*, overhung by copper beech and weeping ash.

Near the front door of the house, in what must once have been a small courtyard, is the sunken rose garden. Here there is a fine display of *Rosa* 'Madame Pierre Ogen', *R.* 'Elizabeth of Glamis', *R.* 'Cardinal' and *R.* 'Fancy', among others; the pink masonry of the wall behind is complemented by the actinidia's mass of pink-flushed foliage.

A vaulted passageway leads from here to a sheltered courtyard overlooked on two sides by the windows of the house and dominated by the picturesque clock tower of the nearby chapel. A conservatory stood here once, but after it collapsed it was replaced by a swimming pool surrounded by stepped stone slabs. They were interspersed with plants carefully chosen for their sculptural forms or interesting foliage, such as *Acer palmatum* 'Dissectum Atropurpureum', *Juniperus horizontalis*, *Hydrangea petiolaris*, *Erica arborea*, *Phormium tenax*, actinidia again and various hostas, irises and geraniums. The letters P.K. on the masonry wall stand for Patrick Kinnaird, who became the first Lord Kinnaird in 1680. Although the house dates from the early nineteenth century, the Kinnaird family have lived in the area since about 1400.

Some distance from the house, beyond the old walled vegetable garden, is the arboretum, begun in mid-Victorian times when tree collections became fashionable; among its mighty trees, many of which were planted to commemorate family events or historical occasions, are a Spanish chestnut (*Castania sativa*) over a hundred feet high, a Douglas fir grown from seed brought back by David Douglas (it was planted in 1833, making it almost as old as the one at Scone), and an *Abies alba*, also topping a hundred feet. There are underplantings of *Rhododendron arboreum*, although in the drier east-coast climate they do not achieve

Top: Irises and heather grow in profusion in front of the lean-to greenhouse. Peach trees which grew inside the hothouse when it ran the entire length of the garden still proper outside.

Above: Delphiniums growing alongside hostas in the walled garden.

Opposite: The fountain at Rossie Priory forms the centrepiece of the water garden.

the height and girth of those in west-coast gardens such as Castle Kennedy.

The yew hedge garden is a wide grassed area enclosed on all sides by a clipped yew hedge, as the name suggests. Huge yew archways mark the entrance and exit, and Irish yews flank the top of the path which follows the line of the central axis, running down a slope and a flight of stone steps bordered by globe-like yews. This path does not really lead anywhere, and the main axis in this part of the gardens runs directly across it, through the two yew arches and into the water garden. The yew hedges originally enclosed a Dutch garden and later a rose garden, but after the Second World War, when it was decided that the cost of maintenance was too high, the area was put to grass and it now seems to lack a sense of identity. This enclosed area serves primarily as an ante-room to Rossie's most important feature – the water garden – and the second yew arch acts both as an entrance and a frame to the centrepiece, the fountain. Dating from about 1820, the fountain springs from a wide stone dish on a pedestal in the middle of a lily pond, and a little waterfall splashes down from a group of rocks above and behind it. The whole system is gravity-fed from a natural spring, and the fact that it is still working so well today testifies to the ingenuity and skill of the nineteenth-century craftsmen who constructed it.

Over the past ten years Mr Chalmers, the head gardener, and Lady Kinnaird have introduced more colour and interest into the water garden. Where once only ferns grew, a host of pink, blue and yellow candelabra primulas (which flower in May and June), stunning blue meconopsis, oriental poppies, geraniums, hostas, spiraea, *Rosa pimpinellifolia* (or 'Scotch Rose'), gunnera, *Olearia × haastii*, ligularia, rodgersia, astilbe and many other water-loving plants now cluster round the pond, where their colours are reflected. Sadly, the weeping elm, whose delicate pendulous branches stand out against the trees in the background, is dying. *Cotoneaster microphyllus* sprays its foliage across the rockface by the

waterfall, and beside it are a specimen hawthorn cultivar and a *Mahonia bealei*, a rare relation of *Mahonia japonica*. The whole group is set into relief by the darker tones of a purple hazel behind.

A pair of ornate cast-iron gates with a bell-pull mark the entrance to the province that once was exclusively the gardener's – the walled garden – but Lady Kinnaird herself does much of the gardening today, assisted by one part-time and one full-time gardener. There is a great deal to appeal not only to the eye but also to the appetite here for vegetables and fruit are still grown for the house. Although the hothouses which once ran almost the entire length of the back wall – mainly for growing espalier peaches – have now been replaced by one central lean-to greenhouse, the peaches, amazingly, continue to grow, alongside apples, pears and gooseberries, free-standing ranks of currant bushes and raspberries, and beds of rhubarb. Grapes grow in profusion in the greenhouse itself, along with pelargoniums, Canterbury bells, a white camellia and, on the wall, lapageria, a rare Chilean climber with red, bell-like flowers. In front of the old hothouse wall, partly for decoration and partly for picking, colourful rows of speciosum lilies, pyrethrum, dianthus and pansies, delphiniums, peonies, gladioli and lupins stretch towards the gate in the far distance.

From the set-piece Victorian water garden, with its pool and elegant arched entrance, to the new gravel garden, cleverly contrived from the old foundations and enjoying views of the fertile valley of the Tay, Rossie Priory has something of interest for all visitors, as well as reflecting developments in Scottish gardening history which span over one hundred and fifty years.

ROSSIE PRIORY GARDENS are open one afternoon a year, usually in mid-June.

Location: From A85 Perth–Dundee road, turn left at Inchture, 1½ miles.

Brechin Castle

BRECHIN, TAYSIDE

Owner: The Earl of Dalhousie,
K.T., G.C.V.O., G.B.E., M.C.

Standing high on a massive bluff of rock above the South Esk River, Brechin Castle was reconstructed in 1711 on the site of a much older fortress belonging to the Scottish kings. In 1303 it had withstood a siege by the English army for three weeks before the defending force finally capitulated on the death of its commanding officer, Sir Thomas Maule.

Today Brechin lies undisturbed, surrounded by over forty acres of garden, of which the walled garden, dating from 1800, is the most important part, representing one of the finest and best maintained gardens of its type to be found anywhere in Scotland. It lies some distance from the castle itself, and the present owner, the Earl of Dalhousie, who is descended from the Maule family, has done much to improve the link between the garden and the house. By cutting paths through the woodland and brightening them with azaleas and large-leaved rhododendrons, he has made the walk from one to the other a pleasure in itself as well as a foretaste of the delights ahead.

Slightly over thirteen acres in extent, the walled garden has a rather curious heart-shaped plan which has inspired comment, not all of it complimentary, since the time it was first laid out. In a letter dated 27 June 1802, Sir William Forbes (a friend of the owner, who was descended from Sir Thomas Maule) writes disparagingly of the garden, 'the whole being laid out in sweeps and curves . . . produce[s] the most monotonous effect . . .', and on questioning the gardener responsible for the

design as to the reason for its layout, he received the answer that it was necessary, 'not only to gratify the palate, but also to please the eye'; the writer adds somewhat drily, 'to this observation I made no answer.'

One's first impression of the walled garden is certainly not one of monotony. The walls on either side of the ornate entrance gate are adorned with beautiful roses such as *Rosa foetida* 'Bicolor', sometimes known as 'Austrian Copper', with its yellow-centred coppery-red flowers, and *Rosa ecae*, a dainty shrub named after the initials of the wife of a Dr Aitchison, who introduced the plant in 1880 from Afghanistan. The nearby tree peonies are stunning in early summer, when their white, purple and pink flowers stand out dramatically against their sculptural leaves. Nearby is a *Cytisus battandieri*, a tall shrub which belongs to the broom family though its leaves look more like laburnum. *Clematis* 'Etoile Rose', an unusual pink-flowered hybrid, is seen to perfection against the grey masonry of the wall behind.

The main axis, a wide gravel path, is punctuated by a series of individual features, the first being four tall and dramatic Lawson's cypress trees. If one turns away momentarily from the path, however, a gap in the castel-

Right: A glimpse from the main walk down cherub-flanked steps to the circular pond below: the design is such that from this direction only spring flowers can be seen.

Far right: Box-edged tulip beds and a low, stone retaining wall smothered in junipers, alpines and rock plants bound the north side of the lily pond.

Opposite: This is the summer-flowering sector of the 'Bed for Three Seasons', planted with flowers representative of summer and separated from the other two sections by conifers.

lated yew hedge to the left allows a glimpse down a cherub-flanked flight of steps to a circular pool on a lower level. To the right, a path leads to a drinking fountain in an alcove inscribed 'Drink and be Thankful'. Behind the little door next to it – an invitation to be curious – in one of the bays of the heart shape which has been entirely walled off, are the nursery greenhouses, dating from about 1820. Here the head gardener, Ian Guthrie, and his four assistants, who also tend the nearby tree nursery, raise plants for the garden and flowers, fruit and vegetables for the house. Additional shelter is provided in the middle of the nursery area by a huge mid-nineteenth-century clipped yew hedge, its two halves linked by a tunnel cut through the centre.

Returning to the main path through the walled garden, one encounters first an unusual stone 'moondial' and then, at the point where a low yew hedge cuts across the line of the path, two low pillars surmounted by stone globes. The wide expanse of lawn which precedes the hedge accentuates the visual importance of the pathline beyond. Beyond the pillars, the trunks of a grove of birches and other trees

with unusual bark are silhouetted starkly against the dark foliage of the three-hundred-year-old cedars behind. They consist mainly of the white- or sometimes pink-barked *Betula utilis* from north-west Assam, with the peeling bark of *Prunus serrula* 'Tibetica' adding a shaft of warm red.

Lilies and tender rhododendrons such as *R. madderi* are grown in the glasshouse on the opposite side of the path, but pride of place goes to *Rhododendron* 'Dalhousiae', named not after the present earl but after the wife of the last Governor-General of India. It has fragrant greenish-yellow, trumpet-like flowers. Beyond the glasshouse is the other bay of the heart shape, this one open, with a huge well-kept lawn at the centre and in a focal position a two-storey summerhouse, which was used for entertaining in more leisurely days. On either side are two sheltered seats overhung with clematis and honeysuckle, with a fine specimen of a tassel bush (*Garrya elliptica*) nearby, and the small glossy leaves and pendulous red flowers of *Ribes speciosum*, which has been trained in espalier fashion, against the wall. Island beds have been planted with shrub

roses and lavender, along with a small collection of rhododendrons, such as the white-flowered hardy species *R. calophytum* (grown from seed in 1952), which owe their survival largely to the shelter afforded by the walls and trees. Back towards the central pathway there are more unusual plants such as *Magnolia parviflora*, *Trochodendron aralioides* and *Embothrium coccineum*.

After the birch grove on the left hand side, one comes upon a stunning display of laburnum to the right, whose array of pendulous bright yellow flowers in late May is so breathtaking that it makes one wonder why laburnum is rarely seen planted in large groups like this. The next feature along the central path is a stone sundial surrounded by six Lawson's cypress and a low box hedge. Up to the right is another grove, this time of *Prunus* 'Shimidsu Sakura', their stout columnar trunks supporting branches that spread a low vaulted roof of white blossom; fallen petals carpet the grass beneath like the first flurry of winter snow.

Just beyond the sundial the main axis terminates at a stone urn overhung by a hood of clipped yew. One's attention is now directed to the lower part of the garden. Copper beeches, some amongst them as much as three hundred years old, a Balkan spruce and a group of maples lead the way through to a large glade planted with Himalayan poppies in varying shades of blue, among them *Meconopsis grandis* 'Prain's Variety'. This lower side of the garden is bordered not by a wall but by a ha-ha, or walled ditch, now almost obscured by a dense growth of rhododendrons, including the white-flowered *R. loderi*.

The informality of this woodland area suddenly gives way to the formal water garden as the cross axis seen from the upper walled garden strikes downhill, following a flight of steps to this lower level and terminating at the ornamental lily pond. With a clipped leylandii hedge planted as a backdrop below it, the pond is bordered on its other three sides by low box hedges containing beds of tulips. A path leads up towards the steps to the upper garden, which are flanked by a low stone

retaining wall enveloped in alpines, junipers, poppies and *Iris chrysographis*. This path has in fact been very cleverly planted: a group of conifers on either side of the path excludes the view of the dwarf rhododendrons from below and the summer-flowering plants from above, so that looking up from the pond in summer one sees only a summer garden and looking down from the steps in spring one sees only a spring garden.

Another way of exploiting seasonal variations has been tried out recently in the 'Bed for Three Seasons', which has been split into three by conifers and planted with spring-, summer- and autumn-flowering plants: spring is represented by rhododendrons, potentillas, cardiocrinum, tulips and lily-of-the-valley, summer by berberis, hostas and lilies, and autumn by hydrangeas, senecio and dicentra. This novel idea is surely worthy of development in other gardens.

At the top of the steps dwarf rhododendrons, potentillas, *Juniperus communis* 'Hibernica', *Cupressus sempervirens*, ericas, daboecia, phlox, veronica and adenophylla cover the bank behind the castellated yew hedge with a rich variety of foliage and colour as one emerges again at the main gate.

Like chapters in a book, one part of the garden leads logically to the next, but one is never entirely sure what lies round the corner, and one's attention is constantly being caught by new delights — a grove of laburnum or betula, a mass of meconopsis in a woodland glade, or the first glimpse of the circular pool in the water garden. New vistas open up at every turn, and much care has been taken in their planning, ensuring that each area of the garden has an element of the unexpected and a feature of interest throughout the year.

BRECHIN CASTLE GARDENS are open one day a year, usually at the end of May, under Scotland's Gardens Scheme, or by special arrangement.

Location: One mile to the west of Brechin, on the A94.

Above: Looking back along the raked gravel path to the entrance of the walled garden, it is framed by four Lawson's cypress.

Above: The sculptured yew hedge and stone moondial by the main path.

Left: Conifers draw the eye down towards the pond below; only having passed them are the summer-flowering plants behind them suddenly revealed.

Balmoral Castle

BALLATER, GRAMPIAN

Owner: Her Majesty the Queen

Above: The rose garden, where ranks of pink 'Betty Prior' floribunda roses are surrounded by clipped yew hedges, faces west over the valley.

On midsummer days the Dee valley has an air of tranquillity that can have changed little since 1848, when Queen Victoria, on her first visit to the area, fell instantly in love with the 'pretty little castle' which was to become her lifelong summer home. She wrote afterwards, 'It was so calm and so solitary, it did one good as one gazed around; and the pure mountain air was so refreshing. All seemed to breathe freedom and peace, and to make one forget the world and its sad turmoils.' Today's Royal Family must find Balmoral's relaxed informality even more appealing as a retreat from their full and very public lives.

Built of local Glen Gelder light grey granite, the present castle was designed by Aberdeen architect William Smith and finished in 1856. The original building, which Queen Victoria and Prince Albert leased in 1848 and finally bought in 1852, stood on what is now the south lawn. It soon became clear, however, that it would be too small for their growing family and the requirements of state, and the fine castle we see today was constructed in place of it.

The Ballochbuie Forest, to the west of Balmoral – one of the largest remnants of the old Caledonian Forest in Scotland – was bought by Queen Victoria in 1878 to preserve it from felling; it consists now as it did then of native Scots pine, and some of the trees here are between two hundred and three hundred years old. In 1850 the first of the great plantations in the stretch of the Dee valley

near the castle was laid out under the direction of Prince Albert, who was also responsible for creating the basic framework of trees in the grounds. The bridge which crosses the foaming River Dee to the entrance gates was designed by the famous Victorian engineer Isambard Kingdom Brunel, and the wrought-iron gates themselves were made in 1925 by a local blacksmith and inscribed with the monograms of King George V and his wife Queen Mary. From these gates leads a magnificent avenue, which makes a fitting approach to the castle and its gardens and which is of great interest in itself. Among its rare specimens are trees such as *Picea glauca albertiana*, planted by Queen Mary, *Abies concolor* var. *Lowiana*, from west-coast America, *Abies holophylla*, from Asia, *Abies veitchii* var. *Olivacea*, from Japan, and *Pinus tabulaeformis*, from eastern Asia. Prince Albert oversaw the planting of this avenue and of the gardens around the new castle. In 1857 the first greenhouse was built, and in 1859 the flower garden on the west side of the castle and a garden in front of the tower were laid out, with the low stone wall and cherub fountain we see today.

King George V and Queen Mary instigated the next major phase in the development of the grounds between 1923 and 1925. A sunken garden was laid out to the west, beyond the rose garden, and a completely new area was created to the south of the great lawn. More recently, the Duke of Edinburgh has made a large kitchen garden and an informal water garden. Both he and the Queen take an active personal interest in the running of the gardens. The Royal Family spend eight weeks of the year at Balmoral, from mid-August to mid-October. Spring and summer come late as a result of the high northern location (about a thousand feet above sea level) and Mr John Young, head gardener since 1974, makes sure that the garden is at its peak during their stay.

A wide range of fruit and vegetables is grown in the kitchen garden: potatoes, lettuce, spinach, broccoli, onions, parsley, peas, beans and even strawberries grow well here, although the light sandy soil is somewhat

Left: The water garden
consists of a number of
linked ponds bordered by
aquatics, hostas,
meconopsis, dwarf
rhododendrons, heathers
and spiraea.

greedy and demands frequent dressings of farmyard manure. Honeysuckle and delicate, shimmering ranks of sweet peas provide flowers for the castle, together with hardy annuals in the nearby 'picking bed', such as nigella, nicotiana, calendula, clarkia, linaria and meconopsis and various hybrid tea roses. In one of the greenhouses grow blackberries, blueberries – one of the Duke of Edinburgh's favourites – and, surprisingly, grapes (the weakness of the northern light and a lack of sunshine make grapes difficult to grow in this location, even in a heated greenhouse). Another has a superb collection of geraniums and fuchsias of every imaginable variety.

Next to the kitchen garden is the flower garden created by Queen Mary, and in the corner an elegant conservatory which has a splendid display of colour throughout the year, especially in late summer and early autumn when the bougainvillea, begonias and fuchsias are at their best. The borders on each side of the flower garden are a mass of colour, their rich variety of herbaceous plants including the much illustrated but seldom seen Scottish thistle, which makes a statuesque silver and purple centrepiece on the south side. Nowhere else in the grounds is the contrast between the gentle domesticity of garden plants and the ruggedness of the highland scenery around the castle so marked as here. Beyond the garden fence rises Craig Gowan Hill, one of Queen Victoria's favourite walks, which affords one of the most memor-

Right: A flight of steps leads down from the rose garden to the lawn and herbaceous borders in front of the ballroom.

able views of Balmoral and the Dee valley.

The flower garden is separated from the great lawn by a low, dry-stone semicircular retaining wall, whose cracks and crevices are filled with rock plants; along the top are violas and other annuals in shades of lavender, white and pink. This stone wall encloses one side of a simple circular pool and a fountain, which lie on the line of the central axis; a path marks this line and terminates in a flight of semicircular steps and a pair of low wrought-iron gates. Made by the same blacksmith as the main entrance gates, they too bear the monograms of King George v and Queen Mary. They open onto the great south lawn and lead the eye to the silhouetted tower and turrets of the splendid south façade of the castle.

Next to the flower garden is the garden cottage where Queen Victoria would occasionally take breakfast, deal with affairs of state and write her diaries. It is still a very tranquil place, where the only sound is the distant splashing of the fountain. In direct contrast to the formal plan of the flower garden is the water garden; a quarter of an acre of linked ponds surrounded by woodland, it was laid out by the Duke of Edinburgh over a period of two years. Here erica and calluna varieties such as 'King George', 'Velvet Night', 'Golden Haze' and 'Silver Queen' have been planted between rocks overlooking the ponds. Near the water's edge are hostas and aquatic plants, along with colourful splashes of meconopsis, dwarf rhododendron and spiraea.

The rose garden and the sunken terrace beyond are breathtakingly beautiful in late August and September. A statue of a chamois surmounts a marble pedestal sculpted with four lion heads, water trickling from their mouths into a circular pool on whose surface reflected rose petals seem to float in the sky. Serried ranks of 'Betty Prior' floribunda roses, a mass of pink heads, converge on the pool, with clipped yew hedges enclosing the simple composition like a frame. This charming little garden, overlooked by the sitting room of the

Far left: Inside the conservatory, where the display is always at its best in August and September, when the Royal Family are in residence.

Left: The greenhouse in the vegetable garden, with the conservatory beyond.

castle, has a view up the Dee valley and over the woods and forests to the mountains beyond. Next to the rose garden is a high grey stone wall, with a fine flight of steps leading down to the lawn and herbaceous borders which front the ballroom. Scene of many glittering events in the past, the ballroom has often introduced visiting heads of state and royalty to the delights of highland dancing and Balmoral hospitality. On the far side of the lawn is the riverside walk, where Prince Charles enjoys salmon fishing. Although some of the common *Rhododendron ponticum* grow here, the drier climate which first attracted Queen Victoria to this area does not encourage the growth of more colourful varieties.

The tower garden, where visitors to Balmoral start their tour, was one of the first areas to be laid out. Its lawns are surrounded by a low stone wall and the central feature is a stone cherub balancing a wide urn on its head, from which falls a continuous curtain of water. Around the edges of the lawn, sidalcea, lich-nis, stocks and dwarf delphiniums provide banks of colour, while climbers such as honeysuckle festoon the front wall of the castle. All this forms a delightful introduction to the gardens.

Though many things have changed here since the gardens were first laid out almost one and a half centuries ago, the calm and solitude which originally so attracted Queen Victoria and Prince Albert to this beautiful place still pervade it, giving this highland retreat and its gardens a special place in the hearts of the Royal Family and visitors alike.

BALMORAL CASTLE GARDENS are open at advertised times during the year, from 1 May to 31 July 10.00 a.m.–5.00 p.m. daily except Sunday. Visitors note that there is not a lot to see in the garden (except in the conservatory) until late June.

Location: On the Braemar–Aberdeen road near Crathie.

Kildrummy Castle

ALFORD, GRAMPIAN

Owner: Kildrummy Castle Gardens Trust

Above: Crossing the bridge on the main drive it is possible to look down at the descending pools of the water garden: this part of the garden is purported to have been constructed by Japanese landscape gardeners.

Opposite: Alpines, heaths, rock plants and colourful trees flourish at the foot of the old quarry face, the ruggedness of the rock garden contrasting with the smooth lawn in front of it.

Across the lush green rolling fields of the earldom of Mar in Aberdeenshire blows a sharp north-easterly wind withering newly opened buds in the trees and hedgerows. But hidden in a cleft in the hillside lies a pocket of colour, where spring flowers are sheltered from the elements by the crags of an ancient quarry and a shield of beech, silver fir and larch trees.

The 'Back Den of Kildrummy', as the cleft came to be known by the men who settled here, was eroded over countless centuries by a fierce little burn on its journey to the River Don below. Rocks were hewn from the quarry to construct a mighty castle above the valley, a home for the Earl of Mar, who was installed here as warden for the district by Alexander II, and who lived and died here in violent circumstances.

As long years passed the castle gradually decayed, but in 1900 a certain Colonel James Ogston arrived, a man with a vision of how the Back Den could blossom anew. In the space of only eighty years, the seemingly impossible has been made to happen.

A mighty silver-grey stone bridge, an exact replica of the 'Brig O'Balgownie' near Aberdeen, now spans the cleft over a calm reflective pool. Against the bridge grows a Chilean flame-bush, its fiery blossoms challenging the laws of botany on a latitude north of Moscow. Nearby, in what was once the desolate quarry, grow such unusual bedfellows as agapanthus (the African lily), euphorbia, lavandula, iris,

meconopsis, potentilla and yucca. Equally surprising is the range of alpines, heaths and low-growing plants such as anemone, aster, campanula, dianthus, erica, calluna, gentian, phlox, primula and saxifrage. Colourful small trees such as *Acer palmatum* 'Dissectum Atropurpureum' and *Acer palmatum* 'Sanguineum', flourish among striking azaleas and pieris species, narrow paths threading their way between them round the tumbled rocks and boulders at the base of the old quarry face. Warm sun streams into this hollow in the summer, opening flowers much earlier than in other gardens of the area and turning it into a tapestry of colour – a perfect foil to the velvet grass spread like a millpond below. Be not deceived, however: the warmth and shelter of the old quarry can give way to deadly frosts in the winter that sometimes persist into May or even June, and a picturesque carpet of snow many feet deep may lie for months at a time, shrouding the rock garden completely.

In what used to be the old quarry waste tip various specie rhododendrons and azaleas now grow. Old roller stones, erected vertically like the columns of some long-vanished Greek temple, staddlestones, millstones and a rock sculpture in the form of a compass also seem to grow like weird fossilized plants among the rhododendron flowers. The stone collection was started by Brigadier General Charles Ogston, Colonel Ogston's nephew, who took over the estate in 1931 on the death of his uncle, and it has since been augmented by subsequent owners. Beyond the quarry waste tip, the burn runs peaceably along the Back Den and down through the quiet pools of the water garden below the imposing ruins of Kildrummy Castle.

In 1904 Colonel Ogston began the restoration of the ruins, and at the same time commissioned a Japanese firm of landscape gardeners to oversee the laying of the perfectly interlocking granite stones which form the various channels, waterfalls and stone cantilevered bridges of the water garden. Meanwhile, the Yorkshire firm of Backhouses, under the direction of a Mr David Peary, were busy

Right: Meconopsis and dwarf rhododendrons in the rock garden below the quarry face.

transforming the old quarry. All this followed the construction of the New Castle on the side of the Back Den opposite to Kildrummy.

Why the furious industry? One evening, when Colonel Ogston was proudly showing some of his friends around his new house, strolling along the elegant balustraded terrace, the view of the Back Den and the castle unfolded before them, and one of his friends remarked, 'But you haven't a garden!' Stung by the comment, Colonel Ogston resolved to make a garden in the valley below which would, when complete, leave the same guests speechless. The task was not an enviable one for, apart from some beech, western hemlock and silver fir planted by the previous owners (the Gordons), the view that evening was probably not dissimilar to that which had greeted the eyes of the Earls of Mar centuries before.

Although Colonel Ogston laid the foundations of the gardens we see today, they have been enriched by subsequent owners and gardeners. In 1952 the castle was gifted to the Ministry of Works by Colonel Ogston's niece. The present proprietors acquired it in 1954. They discovered that the great gales of the previous year had left a trail of destruction through the shelterbelt of beeches, firs and hemlocks planted by the Gordons, and immediately set about replacing them with quick-growing hybrid and Japanese larch. In 1956, it was decided to let the house as a hotel, which it remains to this day.

The present head gardener, Alastair Laing, has cared for the gardens since 1977, together with an assistant gardener and a trainee and, more recently, Manpower Services Commission helpers. Even with their aid, he has enough work keeping the gardens in their present immaculate condition, let alone defending them against all manner of pests, from slugs and mice, to rabbits, deer and human predators armed with trowels and plastic bags. Although some chemicals are used for weed control, the hardier perennial weeds often become immune to them in the long run and become super weeds because the competition has been killed off. Bark mulch is now being

used as a deterrent as well as the more traditional methods of hand-weeding and close planting. Mr Laing is constantly experimenting with new plants in different sites in order to establish where they will thrive most successfully. Many have not survived, but there are some surprising and unusual successes, the Chilean flame-bush, *Ranunculus layalii* and other plants from New Zealand, and the *Lysichitum americanum* by the water garden among them. Records of temperatures in the quarry garden and the more sheltered walled garden have been kept since 1975, and they prove conclusively that the growing season is, generally speaking, getting shorter. Consequently semi-exotic plants which once flourished here no longer do so. In mid-May in 1987, for example, night temperatures as low as minus 4°C were recorded in the quarry.

Future plans include the possibility of opening the Low Den (below the water garden) to visitors, possibly with a nature walk and picnic areas. Another woodland area next to the Back Den is now a children's play area. M.S.C.-constructed woodland walks and a route for disabled people, as well as a new video room showing a promotional film on the history and principal features of Kildrummy, are all successful recent attempts to widen the appeal of the garden, and a new walk, funded by donations, is to be created soon.

Above: Actinidia is supported on a rustic frame while dwarf rhododendrons and heather thrive around it, but the whole garden is dominated by the looming ruins of old Kildrummy Castle.

Left: Spanning this pool in the water garden is an exact replica of the 'Brig o' Balgownie' near Aberdeen.

Apart from the tender shrubs and alpine plants which do manage to survive here, the garden has a number of interesting trees such as *Metasequoia glyptostroboides*, and a few oddities too, among them the rare purple oak, the Australian evergreen oak, and a cross which has occurred naturally between two species of hemlock to produce a tree with weeping foliage that is unique to this garden. It is these specimens that draw forestry students from Aberdeen University, horticultural societies from France, Germany and America, and visitors from all over the world. But it is also the series of pools that reflect the morning sun in the water garden, surrounded by primulas, hostas and veratrum, the castle ruins which dominate the garden from all angles, the great bridge which marks the entrance to the gardens, and the quiet informality of the Back Den. One wonders what the reaction of the Colonel's friends would be if they strolled along the terrace and looked out over the Back Den of Kildrummy today.

KILDRUMMY CASTLE GARDENS are open daily, 1 April–31 October 10.00 a.m.–5.00 p.m.

Location: From A980 Aberdeen, follow A944 from Alford and then the A97 Huntly/Strathdon road left towards Strathdon. The gardens are 10 miles from Alford, 35 miles from Aberdeen.

Dunrobin Castle

GOLSPIE, HIGHLAND

Owner: The Sutherland Trust

There have been gardens of some sort at Dunrobin since the seventeenth century, when Sir Robert Gorden described 'Dounrobin' (sic) as having '... fair orchards and gardens, planted with all kynds of fruits, hearbs, and floores used in this kingdome'. This was probably a traditional Scottish walled garden, half of it used for the growing of fresh fruit and vegetables and the other half for flowers. The fact that a garden has existed for so long may come as something of a surprise. This is the most northerly formal garden in Scotland of any size, lying only two degrees south of Leningrad and Greenland. It is even further north than the well-known garden at Inverewe, but that at least has the upper reaches of the Gulf Stream to raise the ambient temperature.

The garden of Dunrobin, on the north-east coast, does however benefit from the close proximity of the sea and from its position at the base of a steep slope below the castle. The walls of the garden and the thick woodland next to it also help to take the sting out of the cold east winds which sometimes sweep in from the North Sea. Even when a fairly stiff breeze buffets the parapet of the castle the air can be balmy in the garden, where conditions are more akin to the milder Ayrshire coast than the wild, open reaches of Sutherland.

The formal gardens were laid out in their present form in 1848 by Sir Charles Barry, who was strongly influenced by his visits to Versailles. Barry had already designed gardens for Harewood in Yorkshire and Cliveden in Berkshire, also in the French style, and it was his talent for formal gardening which first impressed the Duke and Duchess of Sutherland. He ended up designing not only the gardens of Dunrobin but the present castle too, which was completed in 1845, its imposing grey façade topped by turrets and spires like a

Right: From the main terrace above it is easy to distinguish the central pool of the main formal garden: it is flanked by *Aralia elata* and box-edged beds of red hybrid tea roses.

Opposite: The chateau-like façade of Dunrobin dominates this aspect but, from the castle above, this herbaceous border is completely hidden, nestling between the stone balustrades of the retaining wall which runs the length of the lower terrace.

French chateau. The castle was badly burned earlier this century but restored by Sir Robert Lorimer in 1915.

One's first view of the gardens is from above, looking over the stone balustrade of the castle terrace, and it is from here that the overall design of the two formal parterres can best be seen, divided by a large central clump of trees and enclosed by woodland on both sides, as if cupped in a pair of hands to protect them from the elements. The contrast between the perfect circular design of the main formal garden, with its round central pool, and the seascape just behind, a strip of beach leading the eye to the blue of the Dornoch Firth, is particularly striking from the vantage point of the terrace. This breathtaking introduction to the garden gives the visitor a perfect bird's-eye view of its formal parterre. Flights of stone steps lead from the castle down the steep slope, which is studded with daffodils in the spring and with semi-wild clumps of buddleia, gunnera and even, surprisingly, fuchsias throughout the summer.

Though from above the outline plan of the parterre can clearly be seen, much else is concealed, and the herbaceous border, which runs the length of the back wall of the garden, comes as a revelation. It is completely hidden from the castle and very sheltered, with a luxuriant growth of delphiniums, hollyhocks, foxgloves and monkshood at the back and geraniums, roses, lamb's-ear, senecio and aquilegia in front. Plants with sculptural foliage, such as *Echinops ritro* (the globe thistle), buddleias, peonies, white-flowered varieties of potentilla, oriental poppies and dahlias are dotted at regular intervals through the border to provide a variety of texture as well as colour. On the wall behind grow climbing roses, *Cotoneaster horizontalis*, and fan-trained apples, a relic perhaps from the days when the garden grew fruit and vegetables.

The main formal gardens were completed in 1849. The most important part lies at the northern end, where trees of yew, laurel and holly, which have now grown to a considerable size, stand at the four corners and low box

hedges radiate from a central circular pond in a fan-like pattern. Between these hedges the red blossoms of hybrid tea roses contrast with the dark green of the box leaves. The parterre is given height by eight yews of various sizes clipped into cone shapes and, near the centre, by four specimens of *Aralia elata* (the Japanese angelica tree), which resembles a sumach from a distance. The central fountain adds a baroque flourish to a scene which, with the silhouette of the chateau-style castle in the background, creates the illusion that a slice of the Loire Valley has been unexpectedly transported to a Scottish shore.

As an informal background to this part of the garden, a mounded shrub border has been planted with varieties of weigela, including the variegated form, an extremely large *Mahonia japonica* about ten feet high, clumps of evergreen *Escallonia* 'Donald Hybrids', quince and, towards the front, candelabra primulas.

Above: The croquet lawn is hidden from the castle by a clump of trees.

Opposite: The contrasting foliage forms of hosta, spiraea and gunnera create interest in this corner of the herbaceous border, a spot sheltered by the adjacent stone wall.

There is also a good specimen of *Olearia macrodonta*, with its daisy-like flowers and glossy, crinkly leaves; like the escallonia, it is a good choice for a seaside location.

The central axis leads from the base of the steps of the castle terrace, past the northern formal garden to the ornate Westminster gates in the east wall; they in turn open on to a private pier on the shore. A gift from the first Duke of Westminster in 1894, the gates are decorated with the Sutherland and Westminster arms; sadly, they are a little worse for wear after almost a hundred years of pounding by salt spray but are shortly to be renovated. Near these gates is another surprise – twin herbaceous borders, once again hidden from view from the castle. Much care has gone into planning the tiers of plants from front to back: ranks of sweet peas on canes make a wall of colour to the rear, bolstered by red hot pokers, monkshood, Scottish thistle, honesty and lupins, with aquilegia and pink-flowered peonies in the middle and pansies, geraniums, dianthus, catmint and lamb's-ear at the front. The canes at the back of these beds are soon to be replaced by Victorian trellis-work. Nearby is a picking-bed with a variety of herbaceous plants including *Lavatera* 'Silver Cup', *Alstroemeria* lilga hybrids, *Nigella* 'Miss Jekyll', and *Godetia* 'Monarch Mix'.

A large clump of sycamore, horse chestnut and lime dividing the garden roughly in two, shelters in its midst an early Greek sacrificial altar, given to the Duchess of Sutherland by Lord Kitchener of Khartoum in 1910. Between the trees and the sea is a sunken croquet lawn enclosed by a laurel and holly hedge.

To the south is another formal garden split in two by a low mound planted with laurel, yew, holly and hebe. Again the centrepiece is a circular pool and fountain surrounded by a low box parterre, this time in a more rectangular pattern, with red hybrid tea roses and echium, an annual from Australia, between the hedges. Because the patterns of the parterre are smaller, and the garden is partially hidden from the castle terrace by the central trees, its impact is not as great as the northern

Above: *Gunnera manicata* forms an almost sculptural backdrop to the stone balustrade of the upper terrace.

Above: In one of the two herbaceous borders which flank the main axis, a wall of colour to the rear is formed by echinops, red hot pokers, Scottish thistle and sweet peas on canes, while honesty, lupins, aquilegia and peonies fill the middle, and dianthus, catmint and lambs-ear grow towards the front.

Left: The Westminster gates – a gift from the Duke of Westminster in 1894 – lead to a private pier on the shore; two magnificent herbaceous borders line the gravel path leading to them.

Right: In spring the bank behind the descending steps is covered by drifts of daffodils; in May fuchsias lend a colourful touch – a surprising feature at this latitude amongst the semi-naturalised planting of gunnera and ferns.

formal garden, but it is rewarding to explore nonetheless, partly because one has no clear idea of its overall design in advance. An avenue of horse chestnut, ash and lime trees lines a cobbled track to the potting sheds in the corner of the garden.

Although Sutherland is technically in the Highland region of Scotland, the landscape around Dunrobin is anything but high and dramatic, and it comes as an unexpected pleasure to find on this rather bleak stretch of coast a remarkable garden. It is remarkable in the range of plants that thrive in this northerly latitude, in an area normally inhospitable to anything but fairly hardy specimens, and remarkable also in its formal design and contrastingly wild coastal setting. But perhaps most remarkable of all is that this mid-nineteenth-century French-inspired composition, so incongruously sited on a Sutherland seashore, should have survived more or less intact and well cared for to the present day. Long may the 'fair orchards and gardens' of the seventeenth century continue to flourish.

DUNROBIN CASTLE GARDENS are open from the beginning of June to mid-September (and all year for groups who book in advance).

Location: Just north of Golspie on the A9 Inverness–Wick road.

Bibliography

ABRIOUX, Y.   *Ian Hamilton Finlay, A Visual Primer* (Reaktion Books, Edinburgh, 1985)

ALCOCK, S., ed.   *Historic Houses, Castles and Gardens open to the Public* (British Leisure Publications, East Grinstead, issued annually)

ARGYLL & BUTE DISTRICT COUNCIL   *Great Gardens of Argyll & Bute*, pamphlet (Argyll & Bute District Council, Lochgilphead, n.d.)

BELLCHAMBERS, P.   *Scotland's Gardens Survey* (Scotland's Gardens Scheme, Edinburgh, 1979)

COX, E.H.M.   *A History of Gardening in Scotland* (Chatto & Windus, London, 1935)

DUMFRIES & GALLOWAY TOURIST BOARD   *The Gardens of South West Scotland*, pamphlet (Dumfries & Galloway Tourist Board, Newton Stewart, n.d.)

HALDANE, E.S.   *Scots Gardens in Old Times (1200–1800)* (Alexander Maclehose & Co., London, 1934)

HELLYER, A.   *The Shell Guide to Gardens* (Heinemann, London, 1977)

HIGHLANDS & ISLANDS DEVELOPMENT BOARD   *Great Gardens of the Scottish Highlands & Islands*, pamphlet (H.I.D.B., Inverness, n.d.)

HUSSEY, C.   *The Work of Sir Robert Lorimer* (Country Life, London, 1931)

JELLICOE, S. and Sir G.   *The Oxford Companion to Gardens* (Oxford University Press, Oxford, 1986)

KAMES, LORD   *Elements of Criticism* (ninth edition, 1817)

LAND USE CONSULTANTS   *The Inventory of Gardens and Designed Landscapes in Scotland* (Countryside Commission for Scotland/Historic Buildings and Monuments Directorate of the Scottish Office, 1987)

LITTLE, G.A., ed.   *Scotland's Gardens* (Spurbooks, Edinburgh, 1981 – in association with Scotland's Gardens Scheme)

LOUDON, J.C.   *Encyclopaedia of Gardening* ('new edition', 1878)

MAXWELL, Sir H.   *Scottish Gardens: a Retrospective Selection of Different Types, Old and New* (Edward Arnold, London, 1911)

REID, J.   *The Scots Gard'ner* (1683)

SCOTLAND'S GARDENS SCHEME   *Scotland's Gardens: the Guide to Gardens open under Scotland's Gardens Scheme* (S.G.S., Edinburgh, published annually)

STREET, J.   *Rhododendrons* (Century Hutchinson, London, 1987)

TAIT, A. A.   *The Landscape Garden in Scotland, 1735–1835* (Edinburgh University Press, Edinburgh, 1980)

VERNEY, P.   *The Gardens of Scotland* (Batsford, London, n.d.)

A number of garden owners publish guides relating to their own gardens, obtainable at the location concerned.

Index